CHINESE HORDES
AND HUMAN WAVES

CHINESE HORDES AND HUMAN WAVES

A Personal Perspective
of the Korean War
1950–1953

Brigadier (Retd)
B.A.H. Parritt CBE

Pen & Sword
MILITARY

First published in Great Britain in 2011 by
PEN & SWORD MILITARY
an imprint of
Pen & Sword Books Limited
47 Church Street
Barnsley
S. Yorkshire S70 2AS

ISBN 978 1 84884 649 4

A CIP catalogue record for this book
is available from the British Library

Typeset in Palatino by Chic Media Ltd

Printed and bound in England
by CPI

Pen & Sword Books Ltd incorporates the imprints of
Pen & Sword Aviation, Pen & Sword Maritime,
Pen & Sword Military,Wharncliffe Local History, Pen & Sword Select,
Pen & Sword Military Classics, Leo Cooper, Remember When,
Seaforth Publishing and Frontline Publishing

For a complete list of Pen & Sword titles please contact:
PEN & SWORD BOOKS LIMITED
47 Church Street, Barnsley, South Yorkshire, S70 2AS, England.
E-mail: enquiries@pen-and-sword.co.uk
Website: www.pen-and-sword.co.uk

Contents

Acknowledgements

I am greatly indebted to the positive help given in the preparation of this book by the many friends who have gone out their way to 'dig into their memory bank' and recall incidents that happened sixty years ago, or have taken time to carry out research and allowed me to use their photographs. In particular, it has been a joy to talk with those Gunners who served in the Korean War and whose memories are so bright. In alphabetical order: Oliver Crocombe, Peter Duffield, Norman Dunkley, Mike Everitt, Shaun Jackson, Bernard May, Maxwell Macfarlane, John (Fred) Perry, Adrian Prestige, Roddy Scott, Tony Younger, and our Doctor Keith Glennie-Smith.

Others who helped so willingly with their own expertise, again in alphabetical order, include: Dr Christopher Booth, Ian Cooling, John Cormack, George Cullen, Paul Croxson, George Forty, Edgar Green, Chris Halsall, Dr James Hoare, Donald McNab, Mike Mockford, John Page, Derek Richardson, Andrew Salmon, Michael Stubbings, Michael Swindells, Neil Townsend and Jay Visack. And a very special thank you to two people who gave practical help in the production; Michael Bowers and Angus Southwood.

Curators and archivists have also helped, not only using their professional skills to provide background facts, but also showing great enthusiasm to share the past exploits of their own organisations: Joyce Hutton and Alan Edwards of the Intelligence Corps Museum, John Montgomery of the RUSI, Colonel Martin Amlot and Captain Michael Hunt of The Kings Regiment, Major Pat Heron and Scott Flaving of The Yorkshire Regiment, Colonel Stephen May and David Fletcher of The Tank Museum, and finally the knowledgeable Paul Evans and Theresa of the Royal Artillery 'Firepower' Museum. All your support has been much appreciated. Thank you.

The painting *Attack on the Warsaw Caves,* by C Company, 1st Battalion The Kings Regiment, Korea 1953, is reproduced on the jacket by kind permission of the artist David Rowlands.

Biography

Brian Parritt was commissioned from the Royal Military Academy Sandhurst into the Royal Artillery. He was posted to the 20th (Field) Regiment RA in Hong Kong and served for three years in Baker Troop, 12 (Minden) Field Battery. In December 1952 the Regiment began a year-long operational tour in Korea as part of the 1st Commonwealth Division, in which time Baker Troop fired over 20,000 rounds. Brian Parritt was the Gunner representative in a 1st Battalion Kings Regiment company level night attack in which he was wounded and awarded a Commander in Chief's Commendation. He subsequently undertook a three-year university course and qualified as First Class Interpreter in Chinese (Mandarin). After obtaining a 'Competitive Entry' to the Staff College, Camberley, he filled intelligence appointments in Libya and Cyprus for which he was awarded the MBE. After a regimental tour at the Intelligence Corps Depot, he did a tour at Headquarters the 3rd Division as the DAQMG (Ops), followed by a tour as Commanding Officer of the Intelligence and Security Group based in Singapore. This was followed by a tour as the commanding officer of the Intelligence Centre and, on promotion to colonel, a tour in the Ministry of Defender in charge of Army Quartering in the United Kingdom. This was followed by a two-year tour as the Colonel (Intelligence) in Northern Ireland for which he was awarded the CBE, a tour commanding the School of Military Intelligence which included the Joint Services Interrogation Wing and finally, a five-year tour as Director of the Intelligence Corps where he became the first Intelligence Corps Officer to be appointed an Honorary ADC to the Queen. After leaving the Army he started his own company, which specialised in methods to protect the Maritime Industry from acts of terrorism. The Company gave employment to over two hundred ex-servicemen and, after twenty-one years was sold to an American Security Company. He was a Founder Member of the Kent Invicta Branch of the British Korean Veterans Association and is currently President of the Branch.

Foreword

by

Major General (Retd) G.M.G. Swindells CB

PRESIDENT OF THE BRITISH KOREAN VETERANS ASSOCIATION

Brigadier Brian Parritt describes this fascinating book as "A Personal Perspective of the Korean War 1950 –53". It goes to print in 2011, nearly 60 years after 21 year old Second Lieutenant Parritt, troop leader, Baker Troop, Minden Battery, 20 Field Regiment Royal Artillery took over his post as gun position officer on active service in Korea.

Looking back over this period of time, the author succeeds in producing an autobiography which brings out with charm and modesty the hopes and fears of a young man, the son of a Gunner Officer, as he passes through school, is called up for National Service and, although he has qualified for a place at University, decides to apply for a Regular Commission. The story of his time at Sandhurst, meeting his wife to be Pam, and securing a posting to the Regiment of his choice in Hong Kong is a piece of army-slanted social history of the early 1950s.

Following family tradition he is pleased to adopt the nickname 'Polly' and in Part One of the book tells of his respected Commanding Officer warning the Regiment for service in Korea and his pride in the professionalism of his beloved Baker Troop as they prepare for war. Life in the Commonwealth Division in the closing stages of the war: the task, the conditions, relationships and the satisfaction of a job well done are described through the eyes of a young officer. With modesty he relates his role as forward observation officer with a company of the King's Regiment on a night raid on enemy positions beyond the notorious 'Hook' feature. The raid resulted in heavy casualties to the enemy; losses to the raiding party amounted to 3 killed and 27 wounded. 2/lt Parritt was amongst the wounded and in hospital for three weeks. He was praised for his direction of artillery fire throughout the operation; he does not tell the reader that he was awarded a Commander-in-Chief's Commendation for his service in Korea.

We must remember that the author, with a degree in Mandarin and a knowledge of the Far East, became the Director of the Army's Intelligence Corps. As such he has been privy to the Nation's closely guarded secrets. In Part One of the book, where he is largely writing as 'Polly' Parritt, he has included a detailed description of the three-year course of the Korean War. Parts Two and Three are a specialist historian's overview of events leading up to the war from the early 20th century onwards. He has added thoughts on the handling of prisoners of war and much on the gathering of intelligence. There are intriguing stories of espionage; even one about an acquaintance who he nearly invited to his wedding who it transpired was a spy! These chapters tell a complex story in depth and with clarity.

Part One

The War

* * *

CHAPTER ONE

Prelude to War

In the morning of 25 December 1952, in an ice-bound valley in Korea, after pointing out the four gun pits, the hole in the ground which was the command post, and the hole in the ground for the officers' sleeping bags, the gun position officer of 14th Field Regiment Royal Artillery said: 'Well it's all yours now. Here's a bottle of whisky as a present. Happy Christmas, good luck and good-bye.' As he walked off down the slippery path I felt an enormous sense of excitement and achievement. At last, the wishes of a lifetime had come true. I was to command four Royal Artillery field guns in action.

To get to this moment was the culmination of years of anticipation. Born in a little remote military hospital near Simla, India, my father was serving in 1st Battery Royal Artillery stationed in Bareilly, and my mother had gone to the cooler hills to have her baby. When we came back to England we were posted to Woolwich, London, 'Home of the Gunners', and each day on my way to school I would watch the soldiers drilling on the square and hear the trumpeters practising behind the barracks. On the outbreak of war my mother decided to 'Follow the drum' and we moved to Shrivenham, Carlisle, Towyn, and Brighton – where my father served in training establishments, and then in a Heavy Ack Ack Regiment trying to shoot down the dreaded

'Doodle Bugs'. When he was posted to France we returned to his parents' home in Tunbridge Wells, Kent.

At school I joined the Combined Cadet Force and was eventually promoted to Company Sergeant Major in the 6th Battalion Royal West Kent Regiment, a successor of the famous 4th Battalion which earned unforgettable distinction in the Battle of Kohima. The cap-badge was the 'White Horse Rampant', now seen regularly on the television screen as the badge worn by the platoon in *Dad's Army*.

On 17 November 1949, clutching a Postal Order for four shillings – representing my first day's pay – I arrived at Oswestry to be a National Service Gunner. This first day was a whirl of shouting and kit issue; it was also the day when, for the only time in my life I fainted. Standing in a dark, over-heated corridor waiting for inoculations I just fell like a log. It was not a gently graceful collapse but a sudden total loss of consciousness. It never happened again but it left me with a sense of sympathy and understanding whenever I saw soldiers lying prone on a ceremonial parade. It was very satisfactory, however, that it was November 1949 as, for the next thirty-five years' service, I could always talk about 'Life in the Army in the 1940s.'

At Oswestry came the first hurdle; the War Office Selection Board to become an officer. I was successful and the next stop was Mons Barracks in Aldershot for officer training under the famous Regimental Sergeant Major Ronald Brittain. (I once heard him shout: 'That Officer Cadet. Right Turn. Quick March' when, as he reached the Guard Room, an NCO obligingly opened the door for the unfortunate cadet to march straight into a cell.) I was also on guard duty when the phone rang and a voice said: 'This is Mrs Brittain. Please tell my husband to come home immediately, his supper is waiting.' I was glad the guard commander had to carry out this mission while I disappeared on patrol.

A guard-related incident brought an icy sense of reality to my anticipated career progression. Rather than spend two hours patrolling with a pick-axe helve around dark, cold barracks, there was a tradition for the guard to sneak into the back of the gymnasium to a warm spot where the gymnastic mats were kept. This I did successfully. Next day a young orderly officer – whom one suspects had done it himself – went into the back of the gym and found a sleeping cadet who was then dismissed from officer training. Next day, his bed had been stripped and his locker was bare. This incident scared me and made me realise the vulnerability of an officer cadet.

Midway through this National Service training I applied for a Regular Commission and attended the Regular Army Commissioning Board at Westbury, Wiltshire. The dramatic moment came when the long-expected question was asked: 'If you do not pass this R.C.B. will you remain in the Army?' I had thought long and anxiously about the answer and, until the very last moment, did not know what I would say. After a deep pause, however, I said: 'Sadly, I hope to read law at London University and if I fail to become a regular officer, I will go to London.'

When the slips of paper were handed out and I had passed, there was a moment of jubilation. Then, sitting alone on the return train journey, I realised that a momentous decision had been made. My future life was now settled, no more thought of law and lawyers; the challenge, the great exciting challenge, was to pass out of the Royal Military Academy Sandhurst.

The time at Sandhurst was enjoyable; it was nearly two years of frenetic academic and military training, with heavy emphasis on drill and sport. There was a defining moment when, following an injury and unable to go on parade, I was required to stand and watch the Saturday morning parade. I stood at the bottom of the slope of the small hill watching the 700 cadets led by the Academy Band leave New College Square and march towards Old College Square. They were in their blue uniforms with white webbing, peaked caps, rifles on their shoulders and bayonets glittering in the sun. It was a pulsating sight and I had the wondrous, powerful thought: 'I am not just an observer. I am one of these cadets; next week I too will be marching. How unbelievable, how unimaginably satisfying!'

The important thing was to be accepted by the Royal Artillery and then pass out as a second lieutenant. With a father, grandfather and great grandfather all having served in the Royal Artillery, and a fairly decent place in the Order of Merit, I was accepted by the regiment. Passing out as a second lieutenant, however, became very disappointing. Having rehearsed the Pass Out Parade many times –

including how to march up the steps of Old College – and having booked our girlfriends into local hotels ready for the Pass Out Ball, the Parade and Ball were suddenly cancelled. It was the first time in history that officer cadets were not to have a final parade. It was also a huge disappointment for my sister Barbara too, who was to have been my partner at the Ball.

The reason was that King George VI had died. At the time, and in retrospect too, I felt it was a wrong, hasty decision and in line with 'The King is dead. Long live the King', the parade should have gone ahead to honour our new Queen.

In February 1952 during my commissioning leave, I went up to London to the theatre with a great friend, John Mitchell, who was a music student at Trinity College. We first went for tea in the Lyons Corner House, Charing Cross – then a very civilized place with 'Nippies' in their black and white outfits serving tea, sandwiches and little cakes and with a small orchestra in the background playing gentle melodies. John noticed two girls also taking tea, one of whom, Pamela, he knew, so much to my embarrassment, he decided we should go and talk to them. The result was that they agreed to join us and go to the theatre. We saw the play *The Little Hut*. In 2006 Pam and I celebrated our Golden Wedding Anniversary.

After the commissioning leave the new gunner subalterns collected at Larkhill for six months' specialist training. Throughout 1951 the war in Korea had filled the news but seemed remote, and the general opinion was that it would be over by the time we were commissioned. Towards the end of the six months' gunner-training, a form was distributed explaining the various regiments which required officers, and in which theatres they were stationed. Accompanying the lists were notes from the adjutants of the various regiments extolling the attractions of their particular theatres – BAOR, Middle East and Far East. There was only one UK posting – Barnard Castle which the adjutant described as 'having good local beer.'

The form also asked whether we wished to go with another officer. By this time, Shaun Jackson had become a great friend. We had been in the same platoon at Sandhurst, had shared a room on the Young Officers Course at Larkhill, and both wanted to go to the Far

East. The rumour was that the next Gunner Regiment to go to Korea might be 20th Field Regiment RA based in Hong Kong. Shaun and I therefore opted to go together to 20th Field Regiment. Disaster. When the postings were published we were both going to Hong Kong, but another young officer, Peter Bates, who had opted to go to Hong Kong with his friend Geoff Freeman, had been allotted to 20th Field Regiment and I was together with Geoff to 32nd Medium Regiment. The adjutant was sympathetic to my complaint and suggested I might ask for a change the following evening at the Commissioning Dinner when the colonel who controlled postings was to be a guest.

The dinner was a grand affair. Everyone was in their red mess jackets and lightning blue-coloured cummerbunds; the Royal Artillery Orchestra played, the wonderful display of silver owned by the Regiment was on the table, and then there came the traditional grand finale when the bewigged footmen grasped the ends of the tablecloths and in one magic tug pulled them off the long, polished dining tables.

Everyone was in a happy mood so Shaun and I found the Colonel from the War Office and explained our problem. Happy he might be, but he was still in control, and would review the postings on condition that he had the agreement of Peter Bates and Geoff Freeman. It was an anxious night until next day when I approached Peter and Geoff who, to my delight and somewhat surprise, said they were not concerned about the possibility of going to Korea but agreed that both should go to 32nd Medium Regiment. This was passed to the colonel and what a relief the posting was changed. I would be going to 20th Field Regiment.

In August 1952, a few days after my 21st birthday, Shaun and I sailed for Hong Kong on the troopship *Empire Pride* . There were four weeks of relaxation and new sights, marred only by the fact that there were four subalterns in one cabin with four bunks, but only three drawers, three coat hooks, and three tooth glasses. It was so narrow we had to dress for dinner in relays. Before stopping at Aden for a swim in the thick, green water of the Officers' Club swimming pool, we passed quietly through the Suez Canal where, out in the darkness of the desert came the sound of voices, it was a unit from the Durham Light Infantry on a night march and they were singing their regimental song 'Hey M'lad you should have seen us gangin'. They swung into view and then faded into the distance. It was a powerful incident, poignantly reminiscent of the recent wartime desert campaigns. Equally reminiscent were the cries of the soldiers on shore – 'Get your knees brown Tommy' – and the shouted reply: 'Why don't you get an overseas posting?' At the port the famous 'Gully Gully Man' came on board. I had heard reports about how clever he was at magical tricks and was a little sceptical. But I was wrong; he was amazing, not just handkerchiefs but live chicks, doves and rabbits all appearing from under one voluminous shirt. He deserved the applause, coins and notes.

A stop at Colombo and a taxi ride for a swim at the famous golden beach of Mount Lavinia, then a stop at Singapore where many reinforcements for the ongoing Malayan jungle battle disembarked. The final four-day trip to Hong Kong proved a little stressful. I had been appointed 'Football Sweepstake Officer' and had collected the sweepstake money from those on board to be given to the person who had won the sweep for the team that had scored most goals. This I had done, and the money was given out. Unfortunately, in Singapore a soldier read in a newspaper that his team, not the team announced by the ship, had in fact scored the most goals. He therefore arrived at our cabin door asking for his money. My friends thought this highly amusing but helped me by explaining I was always away on duty when he and his friends continually arrived at the cabin.

When we arrived in Hong Kong we were collected and taken on the long road journey to Quarry Camp in the New Territories (at that time the new road named TWISK had not been built) and it was mid afternoon when Shaun and I finally reached the camp. There at the entrance was a smart sentry in his shorts, boots and puttees with the red and blue stocking tabs. Behind him was a large silver sign – 20TH FIELD REGIMENT ROYAL ARTILLERY. We had arrived. We were to join our Regiment. It was a great moment.

We were escorted to our rooms in a rather spartan hut with a narrow bed, a chair, wardrobe, washbasin and jug but no running water. We were then told to report to the Officers' Mess where tea was being served. The greeting was affable, and we had tea with cucumber sandwiches. A friendly captain called Bill Miller then told us that in 30 minutes' time there was a six-a-side hockey match, and could we please change and be ready for the game. After four weeks at sea the prospect of a hard game of six-a-side hockey was not appealing, but this was the order. Shaun had achieved a great record at Sandhurst. On the day of arrival there – the first day we met – he had been told to go onto the sport field and play soccer. He had no option but to do this. Thereafter, even though each week we were required to fill in a form showing the sports we had attended during the week, Shaun never again played a team game. It was a remarkable achievement. History repeated itself on our first day with the Regiment. He played hockey that day, but managed never again to take part in a team event.

When we got back to our rooms, Lieutenant Ted Drake who had been appointed our 'Mentor', showed us where we washed. There was a central bathroom but it contained no baths or showers. In the middle was a selection of tin tubs, similar to those used for washing clothes. We were required to take a jug to the hot tap, fill the bath and sit knees crossed like a boiled egg in an egg cup.

Next day I reported to my Battery Commander, Major Johnny King-Martin, a tall, smart, and very authoritative ex-Indian Army soldier, who was sat behind a desk covered with a tartan blanket. He asked me my first name and I replied: 'Brian.' I always regretted this first reply. At school, as a recruit, and at Sandhurst, I had always been known as 'Polly', just as my father and grandfather had been. It took a long time but mainly due to the influence of Shaun, the other subalterns gradually began to call me 'Polly'. Major King-Martin told me that I was to be troop leader of Baker Troop 12 (Minden) Field Battery and was to report to the troop commander, Captain Bill Miller, a brave officer who was subsequently killed in Korea.

At this time it was not certain that the regiment would be going to Korea. There were two sources of information; the first being the 'Popsicle Man' who pedalled his bicycle round the barracks selling ice lollies. He had a fund of information – and, in a secret drawer underneath the block of ice in his hamper, a range of 'dirty books'. He confidently told us: 'You soon go Korea.' The second source was the Indian tailoring contractor Mr Ahmed Din, who also confidently told us that we would soon be in Korea. Twenty years later, as commanding officer of the Intelligence and Security Group Far East, I visited Hong Kong and I popped in to see Mr Ahmed Din, now in a smart shop in Nathan Road and ordered some shirts. He arranged for his assistant to bring the customary cold, fizzy orange drink and then disappeared. On emerging, he politely said that he had just checked on the 20th Field Regiment Account Book and was pleased to say that Second Lieutenant Parritt had paid his bill before leaving. We then agreed a price for three shirts that could only be bought in Hong Kong and lasted for years. They were slightly grey, rough and gritty in texture, and made out of 'raw silk'.

The first few weeks at regimental duty were an anti-climax. After early-morning parades, the rest of the morning was devoted to 'Gun Park Maintenance' and the afternoon to sport. It was not very exciting for an enthusiastic young troop officer to watch four gun detachments spend hours cleaning and polishing their guns. One morning, however, we were called for a regimental parade, the whole regiment formed a three-sided square and our commanding officer Colonel Geoffrey Brennan came to the front and said: 'I have been posted to Korea.' There was a gasp and then a hush. He paused for several minutes, then added: 'And you are coming with me.' For me it was great news. I rushed back to the Troop Office and on the stairs met Sergeant Major Charlie Wroot, the Baker Troop Sergeant Major. His reaction surprised me. He was not at all delighted – in fact he was very restrained. Some time later when we knew each other better, he told me that during the Battle of Alamein he had been a member of a Forward Observation Party, which had been captured and he had become a prisoner of war for three years.

Life now became joyful and full. Each day the guns went to the ranges, ammunition was plentiful; we fired the guns and practised and practised command post and radio procedures. Early one morning there was a moment of unadulterated joy when I looked from behind my command vehicle and saw I was leading four quad vehicles towing four bouncing guns and limbers. A strong memory came back of sepia photos of my father in India leading four galloping horses drawing four bouncing guns and limbers. Wonderful.

Once in the middle of a shoot came the dramatic call 'STOP.' This literally meant everyone and every action immediately stopped. In the middle of the Firing Area local residents had appeared and were salvaging bits of metal from the exploding shells. Highly lucrative but highly dangerous. I can remember no lecture on the political situation in Korea, but do remember a colour film showing the devastating effects on the male body of venereal disease. The showing of this film caused great amusement in the Regiment as the gunner who had been selected to be the medical officer's assistant, watched the film and fainted. Ribald comment wondered how, if he fainted at the sight of a film, would he cope with real blood?

Mess life continued as normal but a little more alcohol was taken. Tea was always served at 1600 hrs and the regimental speciality was banana and sugar sandwiches. Four nights a week we dressed in white shirt and bow tie, white mess jacket, blue trousers and cummerbund; the other three nights dress was casual. It was called 'Planters Rig' – shirt, bow tie, cummerbund and dark trousers. One night a week was an official regimental mess night when all the officers dined. Situated as we were in a remote area, it was redolent of a pre-war Indian Army atmosphere. Apart from those working in the camp, I never spoke to a Chinese person; there were no girls at all to mix with, and only on very rare occasions did we go into Hong Kong. The Mess was our centre and it seemed right that this was so. It is rather embarrassing to remember that we, as young men, called the elderly and dignified Chinese mess waiters 'Boy'.

Two unwritten rules were followed. First, that after dinner on the Regimental Dinner Night, strenuous indoor games were played. One was 'Cushion Rugby' in which you had to carry a cushion in lieu of a ball from one end of the mess to the other without touching the ground. Another was 'Are you there Moriarty?' when two blindfolded officers lay on the ground, clutched each other by the left hand, and with a rolled newspaper in the right hand tried to strike his opponent's head. To the outsider, perhaps, this was juvenile but to us it was very enjoyable and bonding. Senior officers could expect to be manhandled but it happened in a way which did not cause resentment. The second rule was that no matter how much you drank, or how late you went to bed, you had to be on parade at 0730 hrs next morning. Once, when a subaltern missed the morning parade and arrived to find the regiment had already left for a firing exercise, he commandeered the water truck and drove himself out to join his troop. To have been absent from parade would have genuinely upset the other subalterns, but using his initiative to preserve the code won him their respect as well as ten days as extra orderly officer.

It was not surprising that the family spirit in the Mess closely resembled the spirit of the Indian Army. The commanding officer, Colonel Geoffrey Brennan, had served from 1931 to 1938 on the North West Frontier, and all of the battery commanders had come from an Indian Army background. Johnnie King-Martin, commanding 12 (Minden) Battery, had been in the 3rd Royal Battalion (Sikh), 12 Frontier Force Regiment, and had fought in Sicily and Italy; Bill Mackay commanding 45 Battery had been in the 5th Mahrattas and in Burma had been Mentioned in Dispatches awarded the DSO and the MC, and Major Scott Shore commanding 107 Battery had been an Indian Army Gunner. The battery captain of 12 (Minden Battery) was Freddy Newall who, with the 2/7th Rajputs, had walked out of Burma with General Slim and then marched back via the Arakan to Rangoon. We subsequently learned that the reason for the delay in confirming the posting of 20th Field Regiment to Korea was to ensure the regiment was capable of providing the right level of fire support to 29 Infantry Brigade. Colonel Brennan was therefore given the unusual freedom to select his own senior officers. He sacked some and then chose well. The battery commanders may have lacked British artillery experience but they all had a great deal of active service experience. Colonel Brennan was irreverently called 'God' by the subalterns – but not to his face.

In preparation for departures to a war zone the few wives who were with the regiment had to go home. They could stay on in Hong Kong if they wished, but would not be provided with accommodation and would be denied overseas marriage allowance. It was not an easy decision for the wives as they had already endured long separations during the war and were looking forward to being with their husbands in the Hong Kong sunshine. Some time later, a sense of acute, deeply felt, but perhaps illogical, outrage erupted when it became known that the American wife of one of the officers had bought a civil air ticket and flown to Seoul to visit her husband. The consternation this caused resulted in an army order that wives were not allowed to visit war zones.

This unsympathetic attitude to wives continued. In December 1963, when posted from Libya to Cyprus, I went ahead with the car and arranged for Pam to join me in a few days' time. On my arrival, however, fighting erupted between the Greek and Turkish Cypriots and the rule was made that no more families were allowed into Cyprus. Pam was required to leave our army accommodation in Tripoli and instead of a quick flight to Nicosia, was sent back to Lynham, arriving in the middle of a snowstorm with three children all aged less than seven who were wearing T-shirts and sandals. Luckily her father came to the rescue and whisked them off to a nearby Marks and Spencers.

CHAPTER TWO

Baker Troop Goes
to War

In December we finished our training and moved to Kowloon where we embarked on the *Empire Orwell* arriving at Pusan on 20 December 1952. It was a dull day but the welcome was warm. Leaning over the side of the ship we watched the marine band of the Republic of Korea swing up and down along the jetty playing in a raunchy Glenn Miller style. Bands had done this many times and had learned how to please the British soldiers. When the Leicestershire Regiment arrived they played 'Hold That Tiger' recognising the Tiger Cap Badge of the regiment, for the Black Watch it was a swinging rendition of the 'Keel Row,' for the Welsh Regiment 'Men of Harlech' and for we gunners 'If I had known you were coming I'd have baked a cake.' The soldiers cheered and Colonel Brennan, on their behalf, solemnly accepted a large bouquet of flowers from a tiny Korean girl dressed in the traditional full-length dress with its vibrant colours. I noticed the Swedish officers in their grey half-coats standing at the bottom of the gangways counting all the soldiers, guns and vehicles disembarking. I found this a little disconcerting as checking troopships at Pusan for reinforcements was an easy task; how, I wondered, did they credibly check the long border between China and North Korea for their reinforcement details?

That first night we stayed in a transit camp and I was issued with a revolver and six rounds of ammunition. Before going to bed I walked out under the brilliant stars and thought: 'Tomorrow I will be able to wear two medal ribbons.' Twenty-four hours in Korea qualified for the

Queen's Medal and the United Nations Medal. How very, very satisfying.

The train journey up to Tok Chon, just north of Seoul, took about nineteen hours. Given the deliberate destruction by both sides, great credit must be given to the American engineers and our movement control staff for making this train ride possible. When the Argylls took the train in 1950, the drivers frequently stopped the train in order to have a sleep. The Battalion Second in Command had to go to the cabin, draw his revolver and make it clear they should move. In contrast, when 170 Light Battery RA were given the train they converted the wagons into sleeping quarters, messes and cookhouse, and the second in command went to the cabin, drew his revolver and insisted the train stopped for breakfast, lunch and dinner. Our journey was uneventful but very uncomfortable as it was an ex-Japanese military train with very narrow seats. At some stage an African American soldier came through the train and handed out cans of baked beans for breakfast, and to help wash it down someone produced two bottles of Tio Pepe sherry. It tasted good at the time, and I indulged, but I have never been able to drink Tio Pepe since. At the various stops young boys came to the windows with hands outstretched but this did not seem strange. I had done the same thing in 1940 when I had run after troops returning from Dunkirk asking for French coins. In 1944 I had run after Americans asking for gum, and in 1945 I had run for souvenirs after trains carrying soldiers on their way to be demobilised. The view from the train was one of devastation but I saw no columns of refugees.

Christmas Eve was spent in Britannia Camp where a traditional meal was served with turkey and the trimmings, courtesy of the United States Army, but instead of carols in the background there was an unusual rumble. The realisation came that this was the noise of artillery, not in practice but for real. It created a sense of excitement, rather like listening to an orchestra tuning up before a performance and then playing an overture. We were getting close.

Next day, Christmas Day, we took over the guns from 14th Field Regiment, and at lunchtime fired our first Mike Target; three rounds each from our twenty-four guns. The next shoot was rather sad as a young National Service Officer, Second Lieutenant A.J. McBride, King's Regiment, had been shot while leading a patrol and had to be brought in by a patrol from the Duke of Wellington's Regiment. We had fired smoke to provide cover, but Alan McBride died.

CHAPTER THREE

Before Baker Troop Arrived

The Commonwealth in Battle
June 1950 to December 1952

When Baker Troop entered the war it was in its final phase. On 25 June 1950, North Korean forces had crossed the 38th Parallel in defiance of international agreements and had forced the South Korean Army south. Within 48 hours, at the urging of the United States, and in the absence of the USSR who were boycotting the Council, the United Nations agreed to support South Korea and twenty-two states promised to send contingents. It was a unique United Nations military operation, which has never been repeated. General Douglas Macarthur, supreme commander in Japan, was appointed commander in chief of all the naval, land and air contingents placed at the United Nations' disposal, and within days American units moved from Japan, and British and Australian ships entered Korean waters. The first British casualties of the war were on the 2 July 1950, on board HMS *Jamaica*, a Crown Colony class cruiser. Sailing close off the coast, HMS *Jamaica* encountered four North Korean MTBs escorting a clutch of fishing trawlers. They opened fire and sank all the Motor Torpedo Boats and three of the trawlers, but were then engaged by shellfire from the shore, thought to be from a T-34 tank. In a million-to-one chance a shell hit the 'out- after- mast' and exploded like an air-burst shell. One sailor was killed, two soldiers from the Middlesex Regiment, and three from 58 Medium Regiment RA – Sergeant F. Mersh, Gunner R. Barwick and Gunner K Jepson. The soldiers were on board for what was thought to be a gentle 'recreational voyage' and were on deck helping to carry shells when they were struck by shell splinters and killed. They were buried at sea next day. The Navy had responded with amazing speed to the outbreak of the War and before the end of June, HMS *Belfast,* HMS *Jamaica,* HMS *Consort,* HMS *Cossack,* HMS *Alacrity,* HMS *Black Swan* and HM Hospital Ship *Maine* (carrying surgeons, doctors and Royal Naval nurses) were all in Korean waters. On 3 July, twelve Fireflies from HMS *Triumph* attacked Haeju Airfield close to the coast along the 38th Parallel, and HMS *Black Swan* was raked by fire from two North Korean Ilyushin Il-2 aircraft. Thereafter, British naval vessels, in particular HMS *Belfast,* together with the Australian warships HMAS *Warramunga, Bataan* and *Murchison,* and two New Zealand frigates, HMNZS *Tutira* and *Pukaki,* continually engaged shore batteries and provided valuable fire support to the troops in the Pusan Perimeter. Four Canadian ships also arrived – HMCS *Cayuga,* HMCS *Athabaskan,* HMCS *Sioux* and HMCS *Crusader.* HMCS *Crusader* gained the reputation of being the 'Top Train Buster' as it developed the technique of watching railway-tunnel entrances, catching trains as they emerged, and destroying them in the short distance they were visible from the sea. The first non-United States Air Force unit to provide ground support to the United Nations troops was 77 Squadron of the Royal Australian Air Force. This squadron, which had achieved a great reputation for heroism and skill in the battles of New Guinea in the Second World War, was based in Japan on 'occupation duties', and was preparing to return to Australia. The men were equipped with P-51 Mustang aircraft, and on 2 July, exactly one week after the invasion, they were in action over the Pusan Perimeter. With their long-range capability, they were used initially to protect the B-26 US bombers, but then became famous for their success in destroying tanks and railway engines, and strafing enemy positions close to the forward positions. On 7 July Squadron Leader Graham Strout led his section of three Mustangs in a low-level rocket attack on the railway station at Samchok; his plane swooped down on the target but was hit by enemy fire, burst into flames and crashed. Squadron Leader Graham Strout was the first Australian and first member of the Commonwealth forces to lose his life in the protection of South Korea. By the end of August the Squadron had flown 1,745 hours of combat missions, destroyed thirty-five tanks and a great deal of railway rolling stock. There was a poignant story when Flight Lieutenant Gordon Harvey was hit by flak in a sweep over Pyongyang and was seen to make a crash landing by slithering along the ice. His friends watched him leap from the plane and run towards a haystack. It was not a good situation for him to be in; 150 miles from our troops and armed only with his revolver. Attempts to get a helicopter to pick him up that day failed, so next day four Mustangs from his squadron escorted a helicopter and circled the site for several hours but there was no trace of the lost pilot. Rumours spread that he had been shot because he had been escorting bombers who had severely attacked Pyongyang. It was with great joy therefore that in December 1951, in the exchange of prisoner of war lists, Gordon Harvey was shown to be a prisoner. In 1951 the squadron was re-equipped with Gloster Meteor jet fighters that, while no match for the MIG-15 fighters flown by Russian and Chinese pilots, became the most successful rocket-firing ground-attack squadron in the United Nations Korean Air Command. The change in tactics was extremely effective but it did result in more casualties, and in May 1952 four pilots were lost. The Chinese became very concerned about these rocket attacks and dedicated much effort to improving their anti-aircraft capability. One trick was to place a large boulder in the middle of the road and hang netting round the sides to represent a tank. They then placed hidden machine guns on either side of the 'tank' so that when the fighters swept down along the road for a shoot, they encountered fire before and after their attack.

The other Commonwealth Air Force which joined in the war was 2 Squadron of the South African Air Force. On 4 August the South African Government decided that a fighter squadron with its ground personnel would go to Korea and be manned on a volunteer basis. Under the command of the Second World War ace pilot Commandant S.V.B. Theron, DSO DFC AFC, the Squadron known as the 'Flying Cheetahs' arrived in Korea on 19 November 1950 and the same day, flying Mustangs took part in their first mission. Throughout the war, first in Mustangs and then in Sabres, the South Africans were continually employed in the ground attack role, and were therefore extremely vulnerable to ground fire. In the first week of February three pilots were lost while strafing enemy vehicles, and in July the squadron lost six aircraft. Great efforts were made to rescue downed pilots and on 11 May Lieutenant V.R. Krugar was hit by ground fire after a strafing attack but managed to bale out suffering severe burns and a dislocated shoulder in the process. The mission leader, Major J.P. Blaauw, sent the other two planes in his flight back to organise a rescue while he remained circling over the crash site. Eventually, his fuel ran out and rather than abandon his pilot, he belly landed his aircraft next to Lieutenant Krugar and, although suffering himself from cuts and bruises, ran over to give first aid. An hour later a rescue helicopter arrived and both pilots were flown to safety. Not surprisingly Major Blaauw was awarded the Silver Star for his bravery.

The first United Nations ground forces to arrive in Korea came from the US 24th Infantry Division stationed in Japan and commanded by Major General W. Dean. They were given four hours notice to move, were not at War Establishment strength and most were young soldiers without combat experience. When they arrived in Korea they were rushed out to the perimeter of the defensive line around Pusan in support of the South Korean Army and, although heavily outnumbered and suffering severe casualties, they held the North Korean advance until reinforcements arrived. It was a desperate battle and initially it seemed very likely that the whole force would be pushed back into the sea. The North Koreans had the advantage of being able to concentrate their forces to attack at any point in the perimeter, and Lieutenant General W.H. Walker, in command of the defence, had to continually move his meagre reserves to meet every fresh attack. As Wellington had said about the Battle of Waterloo, 'It was a very close run thing'.

Prime Minister Atlee had decided to send ground forces to Korea in support of the United Nations Resolution and on the principle a 'Platoon now is better than a company later', it was decided to send 27 Infantry Brigade which was sitting peacefully in Hong Kong. It had been intended to send 29 Infantry Brigade but this was still forming up in the UK and would not be available to help in the critical battles around Pusan. On 20 August 1950, Brigadier Basil A.

Coad DSO, late Wiltshire Regiment, was therefore told to move his Brigade to Pusan. The commanding officers of the 1st Battalion Middlesex Regiment and 1st Battalion Argyll and Sutherland Highlanders were told of the move at 0900 hrs on 21 August, and on 25 August, together with the Brigade Headquarter, boarded HMS *Unicorn* and HMS *Ceylon*. On their way to Korea, in a very nice gesture, the Captain of the *Ceylon* ordered that the Argyle's Battalion Flag should be flown in addition to the White Ensign which, the sailors claimed at the time, was 'unique in naval history'. For artillery support they had four 17 Pdr Anti Tank guns of A Troop 27 (Dragon) Battery RA consisting of three officers and fifty-seven gunners, although on their arrival in Korea they were quickly re-equipped with 4.2 inch mortars which were considered more appropriate for the coming battles. Also sent, but not as part of 27 Brigade, was Baker Troop of 267 Combined Operations Bombardment Battery RA which successfully co-ordinated fire from the Royal Naval ships. There was no armoured support and the Brigade was totally reliant on the willingness and generosity of the American Army for transport, clothing and spares. For this reason it became known as the 'Woolworth Brigade' because everything was 'on the cheap'. There was a Provost Section, a Field Cash Office, a REME Light Aid Detachment and a small Ordnance Field Park. The Indian Army responded for medical with amazing speed and sent their 60th (Indian) Parachute Field Ambulance. During the next four months of battle the handicap of being sent as a 'token force' and not being 'self-contained logistically' makes the achievements of this hastily collected Brigade remarkable.

Three weeks after their arrival, on 5 September, the Brigade went into action for the first time as part of the Breakout Force from the Pusan Perimeter. The plan was that this breakout would be coordinated with an amphibious landing in the north at Inchon, and 27 Brigade's objectives were the enemy positions along the Naktong River and the town of Sonju. On 21 September the Middlesex Regiment, known as the 'Die Hards' crossed the River and, at the point of the bayonet, first captured the feature known as 'Plum Pudding' and then a much more difficult position, which became known as 'Middlesex Hill'. The mountains in the central region are

3,000 feet high, are all razor-backed, covered in scrub, and often very difficult to climb for the last hundred feet or so; it meant the soldiers often having to sling their rifles and scramble up with both hands. The Argylls moved towards Sonju, encountered stiff opposition, and were heavily mortared but, supported by five US Sherman tanks commanded by the American 'Tankie' Major K.W. Koch, reached their objectives. Because of the number of casualties, Major Kenneth Muir, the second in command of the battalion, undertook the task of leading the stretcher-bearers up to the top of the hill and, with complete disregard for his own safety while under continuous fire, moved round encouraging the soldiers and organising the defence. Unfortunately, the US Army Artillery unit that had been promised to support the Argylls was removed and a request was made for air support. Eventually, three Mustang fighter aircraft appeared overhead but, in spite of the recognition panels that had been laid out, in a tragic mistake; the Mustangs dropped napalm bombs on the forward Company. These bombs, each filled with 110 gallons of a mixture of sodium palminate and gasoline, formed a gelatine liquid that spread over an area of about half an acre and burned with a 1,000-degree heat. Lieutenant Colonel G.I. Malcolm has described the scene: 'The whole surprising tragedy was over in two minutes leaving the top of the hill a sea of fire which threatened to destroy both fit and wounded alike. The ridge became quite untenable; the irreplaceable reserve of ammunition was exploding everywhere in the flames and the majority of the defenders were forced to escape by plunging down the sheer slope.' Major Kenneth Muir was determined that the hill should not be lost to the enemy, so rounded up some thirty men and led them with a cheer back to the smouldering top in a hail of fire. The North Koreans were now firing from three sides, and Major Muir, together with Major Gordon-Ingram, picked up a light mortar and brought it into action. It was at this moment a burst of machine gun fire hit Major Muir and he was killed. For this remarkable display of leadership and bravery, Major Muir, aged thirty-eight, was subsequently awarded a very well-deserved Victoria Cross.

The American Air Force held a detailed enquiry into the incident and the 93rd Bombardment Wing made a very generous donation to the families of those killed and wounded in the incident. When writing back to acknowledge the cheque, Lieut General Sir Gordon Macmillan, the Colonel of the regiment, wrote: 'The Regiment's friendship with the United States Air Force personnel can never be impaired by having suffered on one occasion from the risks which are inseparable from operations in modern war.' The South Korean Government were so impressed by the fighting of the Argylls and the Middlesex Regiment at the Naktong River that they awarded the Brigade a 'Korean Presidential Unit Citation', a colourful brooch to be worn on the upper right arm and representing the 'Ying and the Yang' design of the Korean flag. The UK Government, however, banned the wearing of this citation on the grounds they had no way of responding to the South Korean Army. The citation document was to be presented to the Argylls by General Walker, but on his way to the parade he was killed in a traffic accident and General Milburn gave the award which is now framed and hanging in the Argylls' Regimental Museum. The South Korean Government also awarded a second Presidential Unit Citation at this time, not for gallantry, but for humanitarian reasons. It went to H.M. Hospital Ship *Maine* and read:

> HMHS *Maine* has distinguished itself in support of UN forces in Korea, providing expert and humanitarian care for friendly forces; the Medical Officers through extra effort over and above their already strenuous and full occupation, gave unstintingly of their remaining time to visit Republic of Korea hospitals and rendering instructive and consultative service which did much to improve the knowledge and ability of the Korean doctors in the care and administration of war casualties. The outstanding performance of duty by each individual member of HMHS *Maine* is in accord with the highest tradition of military service.

Like the Argyle soldiers, the Lordships of the Admiralty refused permission for the sailors to wear this distinction.

The United Nations advance north continued, and on 28 September Seoul was re-captured. At this time the famous 3rd Battalion Royal Australian Regiment arrived to join the Brigade, and so Brigadier Coad, on his own initiative, changed the title to 27 British Commonwealth Brigade. Reinforcements also arrived in the brigade, including a draft from the Highland Regiments for the Argylls and a company of the Queen's Regiment for the Middlesex Regiment. This cross-posting of soldiers from one battalion to another became extremely common throughout the war, and those soldiers who were determined to retain their own cap badge were forcibly told on arrival that they were now privileged to be members of a new and better regiment, so they had better 'change their cap badge NOW!' As the rule was that no-one under the age of nineteen could go to Korea, and the Commander in Chief Sir John Harding had decreed that the War Establishment for a battalion of 38 officers and 945 soldiers should be fulfilled, before they sailed, the Argylls and Middlesex Regiments received seventeen men from the Leicestershires, twenty-five from the King's Own Scottish Borderers, thirty-eight from the South Staffordshire Regiment, and fifty-three from the KSLI. The Eighth Roya Irish Hussars also received soldiers from other armoured regiments to bring them up to strength, and these included a number of reservists from the Royal Tank Regiment who were great rivals of the Cavalry. To the annoyance of the Hussar NCOs, these 'Tankies' would select the right moment and then whistle 'My Boy Willie' which is the Regimental Quick March of the Royal Tank Regiment.

Although the Chinese Government warned that they would intervene if UN forces entered North Korea, General Macarthur was not deterred by this threat and was determined to 'finish the job.' On 1 October he ordered his troops to cross the 38th Parallel, capture the North Korean capital Pyongyang, and then, on 26 October, to reach the Yalu River on the border with China. The 27th Brigade was fully committed in this advance and there was a delightful moment when the leading platoon of the Argylls entered the town of Saiwon and found themselves in the middle of a North Korean column retreating north. The Koreans had never before seen Scottish soldiers wearing their regimental hats known as 'balmorals' and, confusing their identity, asked, 'Russky?' The platoon commander, with great presence of mind realising the mistake, responded with appropriate Scottish noises. Cigarettes were exchanged, and a Korean girl soldier climbed into the platoon commander's jeep and warmly suggested an exchange of hats. Sadly, however, a nearby American soldier who was also asked 'Russky?' evidently replied 'Hell no' and there was a rapid dispersal of all concerned. Luckily, the platoon commander did manage to retrieve his balmoral as the girl had dropped it and fled.

On 27 October a Chinese Army, cleverly calling itself 'The Chinese Volunteer Army', launched the first phase of their counter offensive, and Chinese MIG fighters crossed the Yalu for the first time. But General Macarthur, still not convinced that the Chinese would enter the war, continued to urge his divisions to advance. The rumour spread that the first troops to reach the Yalu would be the first to go home. On 31 October, 27 Brigade reached the Yalu and, as all Korean resistance had ceased, enjoyed a day's rest. Everyone was talking about being 'home for Christmas', but on 25 November the Chinese launched the second phase of their offensive and suddenly, whereas for the past three months the cry had been 'On, On, On', the cry now became 'Back, Back, Back.' A British tank commander with a degree of understatement wrote: 'The withdrawal is somewhat confused. The panic button has been pressed and some troops have practically got to Japan.' The Chinese drove relentlessly forward, eventually recapturing Pyongyang and Seoul, and by the New Year the Brigade was back south of the Han River to a North Korean Defensive Line they had captured three months before.

In the press, great emphasis had been given to the sad tales of the retreat, but the story of 27 Commonwealth Brigade is not one of 'bug out' and panic. Orders and counter-orders became the routine, but the withdrawal was controlled and co-ordinated, and the brigade was often selected by the divisional commander to act as a stabilising rearguard force. The three battalions, established defensive positions, dug in and held their ground until the order came to retire. Given the shortage of infantry at one stage, Captain John Cormack RE had earned a well-deserved MC for converting his sapper troops into infantry and fighting from slit trenches.

In November the soldiers of 27 Brigade were still wearing their thin tropical jungle-green tunics, trousers and floppy hats when, without notice, the wind changed north and temperatures dropped to 25 degrees of frost, then to 45 degrees of frost. In these conditions everything froze within minutes; hot water poured into the radiator of a vehicle froze before it reached the bottom, water took over an hour to boil, Bren guns and rifles had to be fired at intervals to keep them in operation, and the locks of the medium machine guns had to be kept in a sentry's pocket for warmth. The 27 Infantry Brigade had been a token force sent to war in a hurry with no armoured element and minimal artillery and logistic support but they had done their job.

In November 1950, 29 Independent Infantry Brigade arrived under the command of Brigadier T. Brodie, late Cheshire Regiment. This was a 'proper' brigade with a full brigade staff, and three battalions – 1st Battalion Gloucestershire Regiment, 1st Battalion Royal Northumberland Fusiliers and 1st Battalion Royal Ulster Rifles. In support were the 8th King's Royal Irish Hussars with sixty-four Centurion tanks and eight Royal Artillery Cromwell tanks to provide armoured OP support; C Squadron 7th Royal Tank Regiment with sixteen Churchill Crocodile tanks; 45 Field Regiment RA; 11(Sphinx) LAA Battery RA; 170 Mortar Battery RA; 55 Independent Field Squadron RE; 29 Independent Brigade Signal Squadron; 26 Field Ambulance; 22 Field Surgical Team; 9 Field Transfusion Team; 57 Company RASC; 10 Infantry Workshop; 29 Brigade Ordnance Field Park; 223 and 224 mobile dental teams, and 904 Field Security Section, consisting of two officers and twenty-eight other ranks, all of who were Reservists. They were not a 'token force', but a 'self-contained' brigade, albeit still heavily dependent on the US military for logistical support.

Although the United Nations forces had suffered a bad defeat on the Yalu and been forced back south of the River Han, a new mood of determination emerged in the United Nations Army. On 1 January 1951, Brigadier Brodie, commanding 29 Independent Infantry Brigade, issued an Order of the Day to all his troops: 'After weeks of frustration we have nothing between us and the Chinese. I have no intention that this Brigade Group will retire before the enemy unless ordered by higher authority in order to conform to general movement. If you meet him you are to knock hell out of him with everything you have got. You are only to give ground on my orders. Signed T. Brodie.'

On 21 January 1951, Lieutenant General Mathew B. Ridgeway, who had taken over the Eighth Army from General Walker, also wrote a memorandum to his commanders asking that they pass it to every member of their command. He concluded: 'In the final analysis the issue now joined right here in Korea, is whether Communism or individual freedom shall prevail, and make no mistake, whether the next flight of fear-driven people we have just witnessed across the Han and continue to witness in other areas shall be checked and defeated overseas, or permitted step by step to close in on our own homeland and at some future time, however distant, to engulf our own loved ones in all its misery and despair. These are the things for which we fight. Never have members of any military command had a greater challenge than we, or a finer opportunity to show ourselves and our people, at their best and thus be an honour to the profession of arms and a credit to those who bred us.'

These two documents show the change in direction and determination of the United Nations forces; the time of retreat had past and now was the time of consolidation and then advance. A new sense of realism about the strengths and weaknesses of the Chinese Army was accepted; no one any longer doubted their skill and bravery in the attack, but it was also apparent that in this war of 'lines of communication and resupply' the Chinese had over-extended themselves. Rather like the initial myth of Japanese invincibility in the jungle which was gradually eroded during the Burma Campaign, a feeling of confidence grew that the Chinese 'human waves' could be stopped and defeated; that even if you were surrounded there was no need to withdraw, and the longer you held your positions, the weaker and more vulnerable the attackers became. Chinese road and rail supply was being disrupted and destroyed and even though hundreds of porters were carrying prodigious loads south every night, they had to hide by day or suffer devastating bombing attacks. The result was that the Chinese soldiers were on starvation rations, disease was spreading and the wounded could not be evacuated. During their campaigns against Chiang Kai Shek's Nationalist Forces the Red Army had solved many of their logistic problems by using Mao Tse Tung's philosophy: 'We are the fish and the people are the sea.' There was no 'sea' in Korea, the North Korean economy had collapsed and there was no significant help, even from the sympathetic North Koreans. The Chinese advance, therefore, halted and the war entered a strange phase where the United Nations commanders were not sure where the enemy was or what were its next objectives. Intelligence about the North Korean and Chinese Armies was improving, but as intelligence gathering was totally in the hands of the Americans, very little reached the British units and no one seemed to know what had happened to the Chinese Army. The Squadron Commander of C Squadron 7th RTR wrote to his Colonel: 'This is the most shambolic campaign ever. Nobody knows anything. The Intelligence Service is non-existent. With the help of an atlas and the *Daily Mirror,* you will find out as much as we know about operations. Rumours are rife and worthless.' One officer, who was concerned about this and was determined to do something about it, was Major Farrar-Hockley, Adjutant of the Gloucesters. He requested a liaison officer to be attached to the Battalion and Captain Norman Dunkley was posted to the Gloucesters from 170 Battery to fill this role. Farrar-Hockley gave him a simple order: 'Go and find out what is happening.' Norman Dunkley did just that; he first went to the Commonwealth Division Intelligence Cell, which was manned by an Intelligence Corps officer and asked what the Chinese were doing. He was told that information was scarce but it was believed that the Chinese were suffering from an outbreak of bubonic plague and this was the reason they were not advancing. He then went on to the Corps Headquarter and asked to be briefed. He was received courteously and allowed to attend the Corps Daily Briefing given by the Corps Senior Intelligence officer. Then, to his surprise, he was invited to attend an intimate session held in the Corps Commander's tent where only the Corps Commander and the senior Intelligence Officer were present. The Intelligence Officer played the part of the opposing Chinese Corps Commander and was questioned by the American Corps Commander: 'Why did you move 346 Regiment to your right flank?'; 'Why did you pull back from Point 241 after succeeding in your assault?' Dunkley found it both fascinating and illuminating and, with traces of the enemy positions, returned to the Gloucesters. Farrar-Hockley now realised he knew more about the enemy than anyone in the Commonwealth Division and so went to see the Commonwealth Divisional Commander to pass on his knowledge. It was a remarkable display of initiative on the part of a battalion Adjutant; small wonder that he eventually became General Sir Anthony Farrar-Hockley GBE KCB DSO and Bar MC.

On 28 January United Nations forces, now including both 27 and 29 Brigades, began once again to move north and on 15 March recaptured Seoul. The advance continued, and on 15 April a defensive line, called the 'Jamestown Line' was established along the 38th Parallel. A major factor in the successful establishment of this line was the Battle of the Imjin. On 22 April the Chinese forces began their Fifth Offensive with the aim of breaking through the 38th Parallel positions and cutting the route to the south. It was to be Mao Tse Tung's final attempt to gain victory. The full weight of the attack by the Chinese 64th Army attacking with three divisions in column, fell upon 29 Commonwealth Brigade with the 1st Battalion Royal Ulster Rifles, the 1st Battalion Royal Northumberland Fusiliers, the 1st Battalion Gloucestershire Regiment and a battalion of Belgium troops supported by the 8th Hussars, 45 Field Regiment RA and 170 Independent Mortar Battery RA. The attack was successfully held with extraordinary gallantry for three days, which enabled the remainder of the United Nations forces to withdraw, regroup and then secure the line of the Han River including the City of Seoul – the prize for which the Chinese had gambled and lost. The Gloucesters suffered a large number of casualties at the Imjin Battle but continued fighting until they ran out of ammunition; their commanding officer Lieutentant Colonel Cairns who directed the fighting until the very last minute, was taken prisoner and was later awarded the Victoria Cross, as was Lieutenant Philip Curtis who, in spite of being severely wounded, made a second 'desperate charge, hurling grenades, but was killed by a burst of fire when within a few yards of his objective.' That week, an account of the Imjin Battle was reported in the London *Times* : 'The Gloucesters, for what they have now done and for what went before it, deserve to be singled out for honourable mention. But they did not stand alone. The Royal Northumberland Fusiliers, the Royal Ulster Rifles and the other Commonwealth units, each with a past to live up to, shared with the Gloucesters this most testing of all hazards on the battlefield – attack by overwhelming numbers.' Their orders were clear, 'no withdrawal' or in the vernacular, 'no more bugging out.' 29 Commonwealth Brigade did just this, and the story of their epic battle is beautifully described in the excellent book *To the Last Round*, written by the eminent Korean War Historian Andrew Salmon. The Gloucesters were awarded the US Presidential Citation, as were C Troop 170 Battery RA. When news of the honour arrived, it was announced that the whole of 170 Battery had been awarded the coveted Citation and Captain Norman Dunkely, serving in Battery Headquarters as the command post officer, was given his gold-framed insignia which he pinned on his arm. Later, to his and the other battery member's disgust, they were told it was only C troop that had the Citation and they had to take the insignia off.

On 22 April, the same day as the Imjin Battle, the Chinese launched the fifth phase of their invasion on another section of the United Nations line. This time the brunt fell on 27 British Commonwealth Brigade in the Kapyong Valley, a key route south to the capital Seoul. The two forward battalions were the 3rd Battalion Royal Australian Regiment and the 2nd Battalion Princess Patricia's Canadian Light Infantry. As the South Korean forces withdrew under pressure, the Chinese infiltrated around the Australian and Canadian positions and one of the fiercest and most decisive battles of the war erupted. It was a savage, hard-fought defensive battle, and the bravery of the Australians and Canadians stopped an entire Chinese Division. To give added support to the South Korean Division, guns from 16 New Zealand Field Regiment were moved forward, and the Middlesex Regiment, who thought they were on their way home, were ordered back to protect the guns and became heavily engaged too. In the period 22-29 April the Communists suffered over 30,000 casualties and it marked a turning point in the whole war; mass attacks by brave men could not survive the firepower now available to the United Nations. The fifth offensive was brought to a halt. It was the last battle in Korea for the Middlesex Regiment, and in it they had maintained their long tradition as 'The Die Hards'. The battalion had added seven Battle Honours to their Colours, so it was very appropriate that in 2009, in a moving ceremony, the British Ambassador in Korea unveiled a monument at Kapyong for their fallen comrades, alongside memorials to the Australian and Canadian soldiers.

Grotesque intelligence errors had enabled first the North Korean Army, and then the Chinese People's Army, to concentrate their forces and launch surprise attacks at points of their own choosing. On both occasions United Nations forces had been initially overwhelmed and driven back in disorder then had slowly regrouped, fought hard battles and defeated their enemy. The Commonwealth Division, which had been formed on 28 July 1951 under the command of Lieutenant General Sir A.J. Cassels, was, numerically, a very small part of the United Nations forces, especially when compared with the number of American Divisions in the Eighth Army; yet its contribution had been outstanding. 27 Brigade, with two British Battalions, the Australian Regiment and the New Zealand Gunners, had arrived just in time to help hold the Pusan Perimeter. The brigade had fought its way up to the Yalu and then in the retreat had constantly been asked to fill that most difficult of all military roles; to act as the rearguard when retreating troops and refugees are fleeing through their lines.

29 Brigade was also deployed to cover the retreat and in this role the Royal Ulster Rifles became involved in a fierce fight and called for the support of the 8th Hussars. During this encounter, five of the eight armoured OP (artillery observation post) Cromwell tanks were destroyed and Captain A.H.G Gibbon RA was captured. Later, as a Prisoner of War, Captain Gibbon showed great courage under torture and was awarded a well-merited George Medal. The use of the Centurion tanks in Korea had now become a sensitive matter for Whitehall as there was a fear that the tank's highly secret fire control system might fall into enemy hands. So worried was London about this that they ordered the Centurion tanks to be shipped back to Japan which the *Official History of the Royal Tank Regiment* described as: 'Leaving Brigadier Brodie without his most powerful weapon.' After a good deal of correspondence the order was eventually rescinded, just as B Squadron 8th Hussar tanks were being loaded onto ships in Pusan and they returned to the Front.

In this final phase of the Chinese advance the Australians, Canadians and the Middlesex Regiment had halted one attack at Kapyong and 29 Brigade had halted the other at the Imjin. In all, despite the tense actions of 'retreat, hold and advance' by the

Commonwealth troops, they had retained their cohesion and been a rock in the swirling tide of confusion. Small wonder that one American general said: 'I am so pleased to have the Commonwealth brigades on my flanks as I know they will be there in the morning.' The 2nd Regiment Royal Canadian Horse Artillery provided great support at this time. No British Horse Artillery Regiments were deployed to Korea, but the Canadian Horse Gunners speed in getting into action and the accuracy of their fire had enhanced the reputation of all 'Round Button' regiments. By the end of the war they had fired over 300,000 rounds and lost five gunners killed.

The infantry battalions received great publicity for their exploits and this was justified, but the logistic units of 27 Brigade had also achieved remarkable results. Initially, almost totally dependent on the Americans for virtually everything, the RAOC (Royal Army Ordnance Corps) had 'begged, borrowed and obtained' vast quantities of stores with the result that the battalions, the armoured regiments and the artillery regiments never ran short of food or ammunition. The RASC (Royal Army Service Corps) responsible for getting the stores to the forward units had to cover enormous distances on appalling roads and tracks with very little signage and always facing the dangers of ambush; the vehicles of the brigade were almost all of Second World War vintage and well past their 'sell by' date. To keep them on the road was a continual test of skill and ingenuity by the REME. Things gradually improved, but if it had not been for the professional capability of the logistic units and the unrecognised administrative staff officers who, in the most difficult of circumstances made it all happen, the war would have been lost. Credit must also be given to the American Logistic Units who, out of their own resources and with amazing good will, continually supplied the Commonwealth Division with the means to survive and fight.

The fifth and final offensive by the Chinese and North Korean Armies had been halted; the chance to drive the United Nations forces into the sea had gone for ever. Mao Tse Tung now realised that he could not achieve domination of South Korea by military means and so began a diplomatic offensive. It is noteworthy that on 5 April 1950 President Truman ordered the transfer of nine Mark 4 nuclear bombs to the Air Force Ninth Bomb Group (the designated carrier of these weapons), and signed an order for their use against Chinese and Korean targets, but he never transmitted this order.

For the next two years there was a rotation of British infantry battalions within the Commonwealth Division and many famous regiments arrived; The King's Own Scottish Borderers (KOSB), the King's Shropshire Light Infantry (KSLI), The Royal Norfolk Regiment, The Leicestershire Regiment, The Welsh Regiment, The Royal Fusiliers (City of London Regiment), The Durham Light Infantry, The King's Regiment, the Duke of Wellington's Regiment and The Royal Scots. The 5th Royal Inniskillen Dragoon Guards replaced the 8th Hussars and were followed by the 1st Royal Tank Regiment; 14 Field Regiment RA (Royal Artillery) replaced 45 Field Regiment RA and was followed by 20th Field Regiment RA. In other units, individuals were rotated after a year's service in Korea. Each one of these infantry regiments earned Battle Honours for their service. The KOSB gained the Victoria Cross on the 4/5 November 1951, when Private Speakman, in spite of 'withering enemy machine gun and mortar fire, and although wounded in the leg, led charge after charge against the Chinese in a series of grenade attacks. His great gallantry and utter contempt for his own personal safety were an inspiration to all his comrades. He was, by his heroic actions, personally responsible for causing enormous losses to the enemy, assisting his company to maintain their position for some four hours and saving the lives of many of his comrades.' Second Lieutenant William Purves of the KOSB was the only National Serviceman throughout the war who earned the DSO (Distinguished Service Order), which he did for his gallantry in the same battle. After leaving the Army he joined the Hong Kong and Shanghai Bank and rose to become the chairman and Chief Executive Officer (The Taipan) and retired as Sir William Purves CBE DSO. The KSLI shared the battle of the 4/5 November and earned three Battle Honours; the Norfolks gained the Battle Honour Korea 1951-52. The Leicestershires gained two Battle Honours and had maintained the reputation of 'Fighting Tigers' at the Battle of Maryang-San; the Welsh Regiment gained the Battle Honour Korea 1951-52, and the Royal Fusiliers and the Durham Light Infantry gained the Battle Honour Korea 1952-53. It was the last time that these regiments, named after the area they recruited, fought in a large-scale conventional warfare. By 2011 none of these infantry cap badges existed; out of all the units that fought in the Korean War the only cap badges that remain the same are the Royal Artillery, the Royal Engineers, the Royal Tank Regiment and the Intelligence Corps.

CHAPTER FOUR

Life and Death in Baker Troop

On 23 June 1951 the Soviet Ambassador to the United Nations proposed cease fire talks. On 30 June this proposal was accepted and negotiations began at Kaeson on 10 July 1951. There was a break in these negotiations but they then resumed at Panmunjom on 25 October 1951 and continued until the cease fire was signed on 27 July 1953. During this period progress towards peace was painfully slow; the North Koreans made conditions about the release of prisoners of war and President Syngman Rhee made demands insisting on the reunification of the whole country. Whilst these endless and frustrating talks continued, the fighting went on and assumed an uncanny resemblance to the Western Front Campaign of the First World War. There was no strategic movement and a heavily fortified front line was established with interlocking defended positions, deeply dug and strengthened with minefields, barbed wire and demolitions. The Chinese did the same across a strip of no-man's-land. From these defended positions patrols were continually sent out; section standing patrols to warn of infiltration; platoon patrols to capture prisoners; company attacks to disrupt enemy intentions and occasional battalion attacks, by both sides, to seize hills of tactical importance.

It was into this scenario of two opposing armies separated by strips of no-man's-land and both occupying heavily fortified and dug-in positions that Baker Troop 12 (Minden) Field Battery arrived to play its part. At this time I suspect that no one in the Troop, including myself, had any detailed knowledge of why we were there. Apart from a small number of regular NCOs (non-commissioned officers), the troops were all National Servicemen whose length of service had been extended from eighteen months to two years because of the war. In the first battalions and regiments that arrived in Korea there were a large number of reservists, many bitterly opposed to having to rejoin and go to war after serving long periods in the Second World War. They had established businesses, were enjoying family life, and saw no reason why they should go to Korea when so many other serving soldiers were allowed to serve in Germany. It is to their great credit that on their arrival in Korea they universally tackled the job in hand and provided a framework of experience and fighting skills that established the basis for gallantry and professionalism for those who followed.

The National Servicemen in 1952 were reconciled to the fact that military service had to be done and most felt that it was better to be a soldier, sailor or airman than a 'Bevan Boy' and have to go down a coal mine. It was accepted that after training you could get a posting to Palestine, Aden, Egypt, Gibraltar, Cyprus, Malaya, Germany, the Caribbean, Hong Kong or Korea, but wherever you went the common denominator was to have a calendar by your bed which marked down 'days to do', i.e. how many days left before demobilisation. In Baker Troop the standard morning greeting was for example: 'Only 65 days and an early breakfast'; the next day being '64 days and an early breakfast' etc. This overt dislike for army life did not represent a morale problem; perhaps it was that the gunners had all grown up through the intensity of the war and had fathers, brothers or relations who had recently fought in the Middle East, Sicily, Italy, Europe or the Far East, and a continuation of this requirement did not seem so outlandish. For many, there was a private sense of pride that they were following a tradition and a feeling that on their return they would be able to tell the tales of danger and discomfort they had heard from others. There was also no hatred of the enemy. In the Second World War the occupation of Europe, the fear of an invasion, the Blitz, the heavy casualty lists and stories of Nazi atrocities created a feeling that the more enemy killed the better. In Korea there was no deep antagonism towards the Chinese; it was only a few years before that they had been our 'gallant allies'. There was an acceptance that the North Koreans had started the war and invaded South Korea, that this was wrong and it was the right thing to push them out; this task being made more difficult by the Chinese joining in on the north's side. I can remember no lecture or briefing on the reasons for going to Korea, nor having any formal discussion with the gunners as to why we were there. We young men just accepted it. This lack of visceral hatred for the Chinese was demonstrated when the Chinese began putting propaganda leaflets on our forward wire. The British soldiers took the leaflets and laughed; other contingents took this as an opportunity to cause casualties and booby-trapped the leaflet area.

Life in the troop became a routine and revolved around five places. First the Command Post. This hole in the ground was lined by two layers of empty cartridge cases and wooden logs and was hung with hessian sacking to give a cosy atmosphere. It could accommodate about five people and there were always at least three people on duty, the gun position officer (GPO), the radio operator and the technical assistant (TARA), who translated the target details into range, elevation and bearing by using a paper-covered artillery board. Lieutenant Oliver Crocombe, who joined us after a tour in a Heavy Ack Ack Regiment with its computers and sophisticated electronic equipment, was intrigued to find that we were still using pieces of paper to find ranges and 'bits of stick to push in shells.' The TARA also had to take into account the meteorological data that was passed to us every six hours – or when battles were being fought – every four hours. This was a very important factor in our accuracy because in periods of extremely cold temperatures, changes in the meteorological conditions could mean an alteration of half a mile from the calculated distance to the target. The TARAs also had to keep the record of the number of each Defensive Fire Target (DF Target) with the range and bearing, so that when the OP officer or an infantry officer wanted to call for fire urgently he merely had to quote the number to get the fire support he wanted. For a selected number of important DF targets like the DFSOS targets, which were the targets the infantry had decided covered their most vulnerable areas, the TARAs had to update the meteorological whenever this changed so that they were ready to respond immediately with the correct fire orders. Headquarters Royal Artillery had ordered that

Baker Troop could only have a limited number of DF targets as they had concluded that it was just as quick to give a grid reference, but the King's Regiment liked the simplicity of DF numbers so we greatly exceeded the HQRA quota. In the command post in front of the officer was a 'slit' through which he could see each of the four gun pits. Wires connected the command post to a tannoy in the gun pits, but if this failed the officer had to go outside and shout the fire orders using a hand-held megaphone. There were two beds available for the officer and TARA to rest but, as the majority of the action occurred at night when the infantry were carrying out patrols or the Chinese were trying to infiltrate our front platoons, getting your head down was not possible until around 4.00 am. Even when you were asleep it appeared your subconscious was listening to the radio. We slept through continuous chatter involving radio checks but as soon as the word 'target' was uttered we were out of bed and ready for fire orders. The command post was lit by hurricane lamps and electricity from charging machines called a 'chore horse' which was a very noisy machine and required constant maintenance. Heating in all types of accommodation came from a 'space heater stove' made from petrol dripping through a pipe into a container, which stood on a sand tray. It was very efficient and could be made to glow red hot with heat. It was also very dangerous as the petrol often ignited. On the first day, when Johnnie King-Martin slept in the King's Regiment command post, his stove caught fire and the whole of the King's Command Post was destroyed. Luckily, the second in command of the King's, Major Derrick Horsford, was an ex-8th Ghurkha who had previously served with Johnnie and the incident did not break the very strong bond that 12 (Minden) Battery established with the King's Regiment, both in Korea and later in Hong Kong.

The next important hole was the 'officers' bunk'. As there only two officers in the gun line we took it in turns to sleep at night. The beds were stretched canvas with four iron supports and we slept in thick sleeping bags with a silk inner. Early in the war some American soldiers had been caught by the Chinese in their sleeping bags and were killed struggling to get out. An order had been issued that in future, troops were not to sleep inside the sleeping bags but lie on top. In 1953 this order was still extant but never obeyed in Baker Troop. No pyjamas were worn but I kept on 'long John' underwear, crochet string vest, cotton vest, thick khaki shirt and gabardine trousers with socks pulled off the feet. I was warm and only took a minute to get to the Command Post if there was a sudden need for two officers. In this case I put on a combat jacket and a wonderful garment called a 'Parka' which was made of thick sheep's wool, was fur-lined, had a thick woollen inner lining, gloves, and a hood which could be pulled over the ears. All the clothing had zip fasteners as it was correctly decided that it would be too cold for fingers to do up buttons. The boots issued were called 'boots cold weather' (or as the gunners called them 'boots cobbley wobbley') and were far better than the traditional 'ammunition boots' with thirteen studs that were worn by those arriving in 1950. They had a wire mesh insole in the boot which acted like a string vest, creating a layer of warm air. Next to the bed was a table with three vital items; a mug, a tin washing bowl and a canvas water bucket. These three items went with me everywhere and I got very attached to the mug. After I was wounded the mug was missing and I went round each gun pit asking if it could be found. Eventually it was produced with the unexpectedly poignant remark: 'We didn't know it meant so much to you.'

The next area was the four gun pits, each housing a 25-pdr field gun. In Hong Kong it was the duty of the troop leader to inspect the barrack rooms, bed spaces, washing areas etc. In Korea I never went inside the men's sleeping 'hoochies.' The sergeants, who were known as the 'No. 1s' and commanded the guns, had total sovereign power. They lived with their detachment of five men, maintained their guns and kept the gun pit organised and ready for action. Theoretically, three men were on duty and three men were sleeping, although the No. 1 was very seldom away from his gun pit. How they organised their sleeping dugout was their own affair, although Sergeant Major Charlie Wroot had no sensitivity about this and would storm into any location in his troop to make his views felt. I had a great admiration for Sergeant Major Wroot. Although I was with Baker Troop for three years and was, in succession, troop leader, gun position officer, and eventually troop commander, and knew the gunners well and felt comfortable to be either reserved or relaxed, I knew there was a great deal I did not know. Charlie Wroot was twenty-four hours a day with the troop, would share a beer and laugh, but was always called 'Sergeant Major' by the sergeants and there was no question on his authority. Early on in the tour I was invited by one of the sergeants to the Sergeants' Mess Tent for a drink. The inevitable happened; I was treated like royalty and at some later stage must have staggered disoriented but happy back to my bed. Next day Sergeant Major Wroot carefully reminded me that I should only go to the Sergeants' Mess when invited by the Battery Sergeant Major and only stay for one drink. I knew this was the case but had to learn the lesson myself and never went to the Sergeants' Mess alone again. Polite as my 'rocket' had been, I heard that he had made the sergeant parade before him and had given him a full sergeant major's burst of anger.

There was great competition between the No. 1's as to who could be the fastest and first to be ready to fire. When the fire order came through the tannoy, the No. 1 would use his own judgement to swing the trail around to the correct line of fire; the No. 3 using the dial sight would go through the procedure ELXLE – Roughly for elevation; Roughly for line; Cross level; Accurately for line; Accurately for elevation then shout READY. By this time the No. 5 would have taken the shell, passed it to No. 4 who would thrust it into the breech, then take the cartridge case from No. 5 and show it to the No 1 to prove it was the correct charge. No. 2, often the bombardier in the section, would use his rammer to push shell and charge firmly into the breech and the No. 1 would then yell: 'No. 1 Gun READY.' Woe betide the No. 1 who called 'Ready' and when told 'FIRE' was more than three seconds late. This was not a matter of buying penalty drinks but was seen as a disgrace by the whole detachment. A genuinely bitter argument developed when the No. 1 of Baker Four alleged that as his gun was furthest from the command post the relayed orders reached him split seconds later than Baker One and this is why he was always last. A formal Board of Enquiry was formed, led by the Battery Sergeant Major, Mr Wells who, together with the battery REME (Royal Electrical and Mechanical Engineers) Sergeant, carried out timed checks. The conclusion was that there was slight delay and this delighted the No. 1 of Baker Four; if he was last he had an excuse and if he was first he felt he deserved double credit.

Little attention was paid to how the gunners dressed; if it was cold, muffled figures put on any item they had found or acquired. When we retreated from Pyongyang in 1950 the Americans had abandoned large quantities of equipment, food and clothing, and Brigadier Coad made the very sensible decision that, given the shortage of supplies, our troops could wear any cold weather clothing they could find, except the hat, which must be the authorised headgear. It was the perfect compromise. In summer it was shorts, shirts or not shirts, and any footwear, although Sergeant Major Wroot ensured, however, that everyone had a regimental haircut and was clean. He also made the point to the Nos 1 that 'sloppy dress equalled sloppy gun drill.' Throughout the war I never wore a tin hat, and most times wore a service dress peaked cap. In spite of the noise accentuated by the guns being sited in deep gun pits, nobody wore earplugs and I think it would have been regarded as 'sissy' to do so. The result is the well-known expression that gunners always suffer from 'Gunnerear'.

The No. 1's were also responsible for stacking the ammunition around the gun so that whatever type of shell was ordered it was readily available. One sunny, clear morning following a ranging round, the order came: 'MIKE. TARGET. FIVE ROUNDS GUN FIRE SMOKE.' Up to this moment we had never fired smoke shells and many Nos 1 had not unpacked their boxes. Baker Two, however, who had smoke shells available, was the first in the regiment to fire and was not slow in letting everyone know who was 'Top Gun'. The reason for the shoot was that the Brigadier and our Colonel had inadvertently driven their jeep down a path and straight into the 'no-man's-land' between our forward trenches and the Chinese. Sod's Law came into play, and in their haste to retreat, the jeep came off the road and it became necessary to send out a recovery vehicle. Smoke was ordered to cover this operation and was successful; it failed however to cover the embarrassment of the two senior officers. Smoke was also used to cover the evacuation of a Centurion tank that had broken down in a forward position. This caused a great deal of excitement at the time, as the Centurion was a new weapon and there was deep anxiety it might fall into Chinese hands.

The next visiting place was the Officers' Mess Tent. As there were only seven officers based at the gun line, it was not generally a hive of activity but the food was good and the bar was always open. One evening as I approached the Mess I could hear the sounds of a furious argument, raised voices and swearing. It was Battery Commander Johnnie King-Martin and Battery Captain Freddy Newall who were almost at blows. The cause of the anger was whether the 2/7th Rajputs had the right to wear black gaiters. Johnnie, who had been an officer of the famous Punjab Frontier Force known as the 'Piffers', was outraged that Freddy's Rajput Regiment had usurped this privilege granted, he believed, only to the 'Piffers'. I crept quietly to the back and ate in inconspicuous silence.

Standards in the Officers' Mess Tent were high. There was an Officers' Mess waiter; cutlery was always laid out, plate service was given and no one would dream of entering the Mess wearing a hat. Alcohol was always available, although each officer was rationed to one bottle of whisky a month. It was an accepted fact that the Battery Commander drank the whisky, and it would have appeared an act of insubordination if any other officer had ordered a 'chota' ('short'). Our pre-dinner drink was pink gin and onions which was cheap and easy, although one senior officer did complain that the subalterns were putting too many onions in the glass which had an effect on the overall mess costs. The gunners got two bottles of Asahi beer a week, but there never seemed to be a shortage. When we visited the American artillery units we were not comfortable with the system of officers lining up in a queue with all ranks and having the food ladled onto their outstretched plates, even though we then sat at 'officers only' tables. In the OP we all ate together and were comfortable; the most popular item on the menu being 'jam butties' and 'egg banjos' – a bacon and egg fried sandwich. Back in the gun lines I think the gunners were happy to eat their meals separately from the officers.

The last point of visit in the day was the 'Officers' Thunder Box'. Here in splendid isolation high above the command post with a magnificent view over the valley, Ron Weedon, who was gun position officer, and myself, took it in turns to relax. One evening, however, a gunner came to me and asked whether I would I have a word with Lieutenant Weedon as, apparently, while sitting on the throne he would take out his revolver and do a bit of firing practice.

The problem was that the shots would whistle round the concealed 'Other Ranks Thunder Box' which interrupted the course of nature. One officer who joined us arrived with a strangely-shaped parcel which turned out to be a loo seat. He explained that having been through the desert campaign he was determined to be comfortable in Korea. The soldiers had their own 'Thunder Box' outside of which someone had written the notice 'Please do not deposit your sanitary towels in this toilet.' The apparatus for quick relief, known as 'draining the sump', was a tube sunk into the ground called a 'Desert Rose' – simple and effective. It was kept clean and free from smell by the sergeant major going round each morning and dropping a small amount of cordite from a charge bag into the hole and setting it alight. The inevitable happened one day when a cigarette-smoking gunner got a shock and a nasty burn.

One of the tasks of the regiment was to carry out 'harassing fire'. This meant that each evening one section of two guns would move to a pre-surveyed position closer to the Front Line and throughout the night, at the officers' discretion, fire at various pre-designated targets thought to be enemy supply points. Baker Troop would thus be required to do this once every twelve days. It was here that the fierceness of the cold became a factor. The Command Post team and officer had to be outside to give the fire orders, and it was a source of great satisfaction to the gunners that we were experiencing midnight cold outside, rather than in the warmth of the command post. A mug of steaming tea left for two minutes would become frozen to the vehicle tailboard. The guns had to be moved every fifteen minutes to prevent them freezing to the ground and vehicles continually started to prevent engine seizure. We had been warned that the site was subject to Chinese counter bombardment and had received incoming shells. Shaun Jackson experienced these 'In Coming' but they were a little short.

In March, Baker Troop suffered two deaths. The first was Bombardier Ken Alder, our troop linesman, who had the difficult and dangerous task of laying and maintaining long lengths of telephone line from the command post to the forward OP (Operation Post) positions. Bad weather, traffic accidents and enemy shelling constantly cut the lines, and Bombardier Alder and his small team were constantly trekking through wild country. There was always the real threat of walking into an unmarked minefield or bumping into a Chinese patrol, but Alder loved the job and the freedom it gave. Sergeant Major Wroot could never be sure whether they were at the OP or in the middle of some remote paddy field and he had his suspicions that they often found a friendly cookhouse and were relaxing from their labours. On 3 March Bombardier Alder, who came from Durham, had returned from a three-day line-mending exercise and was standing next to Baker One gun while a shoot was in progress. Tragically a shell prematurely exploded just outside the muzzle and Alder was killed instantly. His was the only premature death suffered by Baker Troop during the war and it was so sad that he was in the safety of the gun position when he had risked his life so often by moving through open country to the OPs. I was giving the Fire Orders when the explosion occurred and as soon as the shoot finished ran out to see what had happened. Sergeant Major Wroot stopped me saying: 'Stay inside Sir. Nothing you can do. The casualties are already on their way to the Regimental Aid Post.' It was also tragic that another linesman, Gunner Archibald, was killed when there was a breech premature in front of a Number 3 gun in 45 Battery. The 45 Battery had another death during the winter when Gunner Waller was suffocated. He was asleep in his 'hoochie', which had been cut out from the side of the hill, when his space heater became very hot and gradually thawed the earth around his bed, which eventually collapsed on top of him. In 12 (Minden) Battery there was a similar collapse of a 'hoochie' on top of Gunner Twells, due to the weight of snow on his roof, but when a worried Sgt Major Wroot rushed over with a rescue squad, Twells told them not to bother as he was warm and comfortable in his sleeping bag and would sleep in the snow until morning. Gunner Twells would have been sadly missed as he made the best 'brew' in Troop – black tea, tinned milk and lots of sugar.

The next casualty was our troop commander Captain Bill Miller. In March it was decided that 29 Infantry Brigade, which had been involved in a lot of fighting, should move for a period into reserve and its place in the line was taken by a composite brigade of the 2nd(Indian Head) US Infantry Division comprising a French battalion, a Netherlands battalion and a Thai battalion. It was also decided that as the neighbouring Republic of Korea (ROK) Division needed more artillery, the 2nd US Division artillery units should join them and that 20th Field Regiment, which did not go into reserve, should be put under command of the 2nd US Division to support the composite brigade. Colonel Brennan always stated that this was the first and only time a British Gunner Regiment had been placed under command of an American Division. As a result 12 (Minden) Battery was to be the direct support battery of the Thai Battalion, 45 Battery an American Battalion and 107 Battery the French Battalion. The Regiment soon learned the difference in the command organisation of the American artillery. In the British Army the OP officer was normally a captain and troop commander with the authority to call for fire immediately from his own troop. He would normally be supported without question if he asked for a battery or regimental target. This procedure would be the same whatever the rank of the OP officer. In the American artillery units, it was a junior officer in the OP and he had to request fire from his troop commander who was in the gun lines. We felt this caused delay and much preferred our immediate control of fire from the OP. In addition to the British, Canadian and New Zealand field regiments, the Commonwealth Division was allotted the US Army 17 Battalion of two 8-inch heavy batteries and 936 US Army Battery of 155 howitzers known as 'Persuaders'. Not only did they provide efficient counter-bombardment support against those Chinese guns and mortars which were out of range from our guns, but they also became good friends socially and were very welcome visitors. Lieutenant Roddy Scott was told one morning that he could use the Persuaders on any target he selected and had great pleasure in blasting two gun positions that had proved indestructible to our 25-pdrs. One of their very good artillery officers was an African-American who, one evening, told me of the difficulties he had encountered because of segregation in the American Army, and how happy he was that during the Korean War, for the first time, it was going to be an 'integrated army' and that black and white soldiers could now serve in the same unit and share command positions. At the time I did not think this was something special, but it was in fact a seismic change of policy.

On the night of 2 March the Chinese overran a Thai standing patrol, killing one soldier and capturing another. Major Boon, the Thai battalion commander, sent out another patrol led by an officer to recover the body and that too came under attack and the officer was killed. This was followed by a period of heavy shelling. Captain Bill Miller, the Baker Troop commander, was manning the OP together with the troop senior technical assistant, Sergeant Croydon Onyett. For his actions in the next two hours Sergeant Onyett was awarded an immediate Military Medal. A summary of his citation explains what happened:

> The area of the OP was subjected to heavy mortar shell fire. One large shell fell outside the dugout. It knocked men to the ground and splattered the inside of the dugout with splinters. Sgt Onyett with great firmness steadied some of the younger soldiers who were badly shaken by the incident. A little later Captain Miller, Sgt Onyett and a signaller left the command post to repair the wireless aerial which had been damaged. Whilst the work was in progress a mortar bomb fell nearby blowing Sgt Onyett and the signaller into the bottom of the trench. When they got up they could not find Captain Miller. Still under heavy fire Sgt Onyett organised a search for Captain Miller and covered a wide area before finding him against the wire down a hill more than twenty yards from the trench where he had been working. Sgt Onyett carried Captain Miller into the command post only to find he was dead.
>
> It was then that Sgt Onyett showed great powers of leadership and determination. He rallied the OP party and finished the repairs to the aerial and got the radio working again. He then controlled the artillery fire with much competence. He conscientiously left the command post under fire to ensure that the fire was falling accurately and where it was wanted. His example restored the morale of the men and had a profound effect on the Thai Company Commander whose complete confidence he gained. During this period one heavy calibre shell actually hit the slit of the OP but Sgt Onyett carried on with his duties undeterred. Sgt Onyett's courage,

efficiency and determination were of the highest standard and his leadership was worthy of the officer whose duties he performed and carried out during the most difficult period of the battle.

After two hours Captain Grant from 61 Light Regiment succeeded in reaching the OP and reported: 'The situation is completely in hand.' Baker Troop was delighted that the bravery and professional determination of Sergeant Onyett to keep the guns firing had been rewarded by the Military Medal; the sadness was the death of Bill Miller.

At the time, the deaths of Bombardier Alder and Captain Bill Miller did not have a great personal impact. The scenario of guns, noise and excitement created an unreal theatrical atmosphere where being killed or wounded seemed part of a play. Even packing up Bill's kit and sending it off to his parents in County Antrim, Northern Ireland, seemed part of a play. Realisation first came when the regiment had a final parade at the cemetery in Pusan and I gazed hard at the two graves. These two men were not coming back with us to Hong Kong. Now, now nearly sixty years later, the realisation of their sacrifice is even stronger. They are remembered.

107 Battery who supported the Black Watch were now in direct support of the French Battalion. They had some very brisk actions and the battery commander, Major Scott Shore, who had been to school in France, was the ideal officer to be in the French command post. The battery became the recipients of 'delicious fresh bread and croissants' but a degree of confusion arose when the French battalion commander gave the OP officer a flagon of wine that proved thick and hardly drinkable. The confusion was later explained when the French officer asked if they had diluted the wine to the regulation ratio of twenty-to-one or, as they did in the French battalion, fifteen-to-one.

CHAPTER FIVE

The War Continues

With the Commonwealth Division in reserve, Baker Troop provided direct support for a rotation of different battalions from different countries. Located with the forward company of the battalion the Baker Troop OP consisted to two dugouts. The first was the OP dugout sited on the forward slope overlooking the forward platoon and the defensive wire. This dugout had a narrow slit and was occupied throughout daylight. Observation was done using a telescope apparatus known as 'donkeys ears', the aim being to detect any enemy movement and engage with fire. The Baker Troop OP officer had authority to use his own troop and could therefore use a section of two guns or the four guns of the Troop on his own initiative. If a bigger target appeared, he could ask permission from his battery command post officer to use the eight guns of 12 (Minden) Battery or, if necessary, Regimental Headquarters for the twenty-four guns of 20th Field Regiment. The second dugout was on the reverse slope sited next to the company commander's command post. Here, the OP party lived, slept and manned the 62 radio set. The OP officer would spend the first part of the night with the company commander as it was mainly at this time that artillery fire was required either to provide support to our patrols or destroy Chinese probes or attacks. There were telephone lines to our troop and battery and we were on our regimental radio net, plus we had earphones hung on the wall so that we could hear the infantry battalion net. The company commander also had earphones to listen to our regimental net.

It was not good country for tanks; roads were narrow and flanked by paddy fields, and in one encounter where the tanks had to advance in single file, the tanks were surrounded by Chinese infantry who used long bamboo poles with a crude explosive charge tied to the end as a primitive but effective anti-tank weapon. The 8th Hussars and 5th Royal Inniskillings had had opportunity for movement but by 1953 when 1 Royal Tank Regiment was in the line it was a very static affair. During the day the tanks would move forward briefly to register targets, either with their 20 pounder main weapon or their machine gun, which fired 7.92mm bullets at a rate of 425 rounds a minute. They would then pull back to the reverse slope to be out of sight and range of the Chinese artillery, leaving peg-markers on the ground so that at night, when they moved forward again, they could occupy exactly the same position. Whilst this support was welcomed during an attack, the infantry were not overjoyed when a large Centurion tank arrived on their position as it inevitably attracted artillery and mortar fire. They were also very noisy, and in the winter were required to move forward and back at regular intervals to prevent the tracks freezing to the ground. As a diversion, one tank commander loaded a blank cartridge followed by four tins of 'mutton scotch style' from his compo ration and fired that at the Chinese. The Churchill flamethrowers in C Squadron 7 RTR had not been a great success; the tanks were old and obsolete, and the napalm for the flamethrowers was difficult to obtain and so, in November 1950, all the flame-throwing equipment had been back-loaded and the squadron deployed as a gun squadron. Chinese tanks, when they appeared, were generally used as 'pill- boxes' in support of their infantry rather than for fire and movement.

As we stayed on the same hill and different battalions passed through, it was interesting to note the different styles of patrolling. The 'mission' was always the same; each night the battalion would send out two types of patrol. The first were 'standing patrols', which moved to specific points outside the wire to give warning of any approaching enemy. The second were 'fighting patrols' who were tasked to seek out and kill or capture Chinese. Running approximately halfway between our front line and the Chinese positions was the Samichon River, and dominance of the ground between our front line and the Samichon was judged to be the criterion for a successful battalion.

Before sending out his patrols the Thai company commander

spoke quietly, firmly, and with determination. His soldiers always reached their objectives, but there was an element of prudence in taking risks. Fire support was only requested when positive contact with the Chinese had been made. The British company commander took a more paternal approach. The standing patrols had clear orders about reporting the presence of the enemy and if it was considered too dangerous, patrol commanders were instructed to just press their radio sets without sending a message so that fire support could be called. The fighting patrols were continually monitored: 'Simon, where are you now? ...OK, Simon move to that tree we identified this afternoon ...OK, stay where you are and watch out for mines ...Simon, OK let's have you back home now!' One patrol, which did not go well, resulted in the injury of a RAOC Subaltern, Donald Clark, who was in the same intake at Sandhurst. Donald was on attachment to the King's Regiment and went out one night with his company commander on a reconnaissance to identify Chinese forward positions and seize a prisoner. They ran into a minefield and Donald was seriously wounded; his company commander taken prisoner.

The American company commanders always briefed with passion. The soldiers looked huge in the dugout with their flak vests carrying all types of automatic weapons and pistols and adorned with knives and hand grenades. The final remark from one company commander was: 'Remember Men. Everyone in this company comes back. Dead or Alive.' The patrol all saluted, turned and marched sombrely to the gap in the wire. They did a good job. The Australian company was a breath of fresh air. The briefing was simple: 'OK Mates we go down to the river tonight ...OK Jack you've reached the river, good. You want to cross over and have look around. OK. Come back when you are ready.' Small wonder that many people felt the finest fighting battalions in the war were the battalions of the Royal Australian Regiments.

There was one very bad day when the Colonel was informed that a gun from the regiment was continually firing incorrectly and some rounds had landed on our own positions. A regimental shoot was organised with each gun in the regiment to fire in turn on an agreed target. The Colonel manned the OP and orders were given: 'Able One

Fire. Able One Stand Easy.''Able Two Fire. Able Two Stand Easy', and so on, through Able Troop to Baker Troop: 'Baker Three Fire. Baker Three Stand Easy.' 'Baker Four Fire. ...Baker Four STOP.' Within minutes, anxious officers and warrant officers surrounded Baker Four Detachment. It emerged that Baker Four had not carried out a required daily check on their clinometer and had therefore been firing inaccurately. An investigation held that the No.1 and the gun position officer were to blame. The No.1 received a reprimand and the gun position officer was removed from the Troop next day and posted to Divisional Artillery Headquarters. It was not a good day for Baker Troop.

Another day there was great excitement; the neighbouring Korean Division was under attack and Baker Troop was required to move forward and give extra fire support. It was quite eventful as the troop had become acclimatised to static warfare. However, we did move, we did fire, and apart from one quad which turned over, we returned safely to our original positions. Courtesy of 14 Field Regiment, Baker Troop had inherited a mobile command post which was a wooden and canvas structure built on the back of a 15-cwt truck. Hanging on the front of this truck (known as the 'Gin Palace'), was an unexploded Chinese mortar bomb. It had landed on top of the OP so I had retrieved it and brought it back to the gun lines to became a troop mascot. Fifteen years later when serving with the 3rd Division in Bulford as the DAQMG (Deputy Assistant Quartermaster General) (Ops), I asked the senior ordnance corps officer if his experts could take a look at this Chinese bomb. He returned it confirming it was not dangerous, but that it was a Chinese 81mm mortar bomb. Painted appropriately in Royal Artillery red and blue colours it is still in my house.

In May the Black Watch returned to the line and suffered heavy attacks to drive them off The Hook position. Major Scott Shore, commanding 107 Battery, drew up a Fire Plan which included targets directly on top of the Black Watch Headquarters. When these targets were called, the two troop gun position officers separately asked Lieutenant Tony Younger, who was the battery command post officer, if he realised what these targets were. Tony Younger contacted the battery commander who confirmed the targets, but gave the precautionary 'Fire by Order' which meant they should not be fired until he was sure the Scots soldiers had time to get under cover.

Static warfare meant an improvement in our standards of comfort and food. The Sergeants' Mess became quite palatial and a garden was laid out in front marked by a series of posts with white cord. Unfortunately, the cord used was Cortex, an explosive cord used to destroy unexploded mines. It was harmless unless detonated. Inevitably, one night it was surreptitiously detonated with a loud bang much to the discomfort of the sergeants and the fury of the Battery Sergeant Major. On the anniversary of the Battle of Alamein the old soldiers sent out gunners to collect flies so they could be liberated in the Mess to add authenticity to their celebrations.

Food was of a high standard, although initially there was a shortage of fresh vegetables. Freddy Newall, our battery captain, was, however, a master of exchange. We had butter and beer which were unavailable to the Americans – they had steaks and fresh vegetables that we did not have – our whisky cost twelve shillings a bottle and gin eight shillings a bottle, but for the Americans every bottle was worth twenty-five dollars so everyone was happy to arrange an exchange. There was a shortage of root vegetables but a gunner found some in a field and dug them up. When questioned about the legitimacy of taking the vegetables he replied: 'Well I did leave a tin of potato flakes buried in their place so it wasn't stealing.' Issued items could also be used for more sensual pleasures. The driver of a senior officer in the regiment, together with a friend, took several cases of sugar to the local 'laundry shop', hoping to gain female comfort in exchange. All went well until 'Momma Saan' who ran the laundry shop opened the parcels and found they contained not sugar but anti-malaria tablets. It was a case of unrequited love. Sergeant Major Wroot decided to place the laundry shop out of bounds. Surprisingly, one piece of American kit which became very desirable were the long-handled bristle brooms which were carried in a special holder on the outside of the cabin of their wagons. Baker command post had one, but it 'went missing' and suspicion fell on Baker One Detachment as it had one with a freshly-carved B1 on the handle. They denied guilt. Great discussions were held how to get a replacement and the choice was either to exchange alcohol or devise a plot to divert a driver and then 'borrow' the broom. The latter plan was adopted and succeeded; the new broom was then painted bright red and blue and kept with the Secret Document container.

Perhaps because of the Indian Army influence, curry played a large part in our diet. Sunday was always curry lunch in the battery and everyone who was able would come to the Mess for this meal. But curry was not popular with everyone. Once, when acting as OP officer in a King's Regiment company location where the company commander was ex-Indian Army, I heard someone ask if the chocolate ration had arrived and the Company Sergeant Major in a melancholy, resigned voice answering: 'If it has, then it has probably been bloody well-curried!'

Baths were impossible, but showers were made out of cans of water mounted on a wooden frame and emptied by pulling a string. The Divisional Mobile Bath and Laundry Unit were about an hour's drive away and Sergeant Major Wroot made a roster for the gunners to go and be cleansed. I went once, but only once. Although it was efficient and one stood for minutes under hot water, part of the process was that you handed all your clothing in at the beginning of the visit and at the end were issued with a clean set. For an illogical reason I wanted to keep my own clothes and resented having to give them up. In good army style, as you went in there were three entrances to an 'Officers' Changing Room', a 'Warrant Officers' and NCOs' Changing Room' and a 'Soldiers' Changing Room'. Once inside, however, it was all naked bodies together.

One quiet morning there was the sound of a helicopter landing just behind the command post and out stepped General West, commander of the British Commonwealth Division. He was a tall, impressive man carrying a long shepherd's crook. He looked like a general and gave out an air of authority and confidence. He toured the gun pits, chatted to the gunners, took a 'Twells Special Brew' in the command post and flew away. It was a gentle event; the drama was later when the Battery Commander and Battery Captain became very agitated when they heard that the General had visited their guns and they had not been present. The visit was unusual as very few people visited Baker Troop command post. In Hong Kong there were Battery Commander inspections, Commanding Officer inspections and the annual Brigadier's Administrative Inspection. In Korea there were no inspections; all the senior officers were doing their jobs ensuring that we were able to provide accurate and timely fire support. The commanding officer, Colonel Brennan, visited the OP a great deal but I never saw the regimental Adjutant or the Regimental Sergeant Major – two people who dominated the lives of the subalterns and soldiers in Hong Kong – and I never met a padre. I did go to the dentist but as there was a problem with the electricity, I had to shine a torch into my mouth for illumination while he worked the drill with a foot pedal. The treatment was far better than many subsequent visits to the dentist. Every six months we had a 'vaccination parade' when each soldier with arms on hips ran the gauntlet of Doctor Keith Glennie Smith's Inoculation Team, two on each side, who simultaneously wielded their syringes and gave cholera, diphtheria, tetanus, toxoid and smallpox injections.

Each week we were issued with a tin of fifty cigarettes and bars of chocolate. The cigarettes were useful as presents and helped relationships when in the OP. In today's world I wonder if we could claim against the Government for encouraging us to get cancer? A rum ration was also issued to each No 1 and the custom was to put it in the Detachment Brew. However, one senior No 1, who had gained a gallantry medal in the desert, made it clear that the rum ration was his, and he had the physical presence to ensure this happened. One parade that was mandatory was the daily issue of the anti-malaria pill, paludrine. This parade was always preceded by the cry: 'Wakey, Wakey, Rise and Shine. Come and get your Paludrine.'

Baker Troop did not suffer from any counter bombardment but Lieutenant Adrian Prestige had a lucky escape. He arrived in 107 Battery five days before the Battle of The Hook, and as the action started was running down to his command post, when a shell burst a few yards behind him and a rusty piece of shell whistled past his ear and landed. It was too hot to touch but next day he picked it up and still has it. We suffered no enemy air attacks, but there was one plane known as 'Bed Time Charlie', who flew over Pintail Bridge on a regular basis and unsuccessfully dropped a few hand grenades. He became almost a focus of affection for the gunners who would ask: 'Wonder where Charlie is tonight? He's late.' When he was eventually shot down, there was almost a feeling of loss. There was a Light Anti-Aircraft Troop equipped with 40 mm Bofor guns, part of 61st Light Regiment deployed at the bridges, but given the lack of Chinese air attack the detachments were reduced to a No 1 and two gunners and the remaining gunners posted to man 4.2 mortars. The gunners were delighted with this posting, as they gained no pleasure from sitting around all day waiting for something to shoot at. Our United Nations Air Army was a powerful force with a devastating capability. Bombers, fighters, ground attack and reconnaissance aircraft, all were available to support operations. Watching our aircraft swoop suddenly from a clear sky to napalm Chinese positions just in front of our forward trenches was an awe-inspiring and frightening sight; the reaction was not elation but rather 'Poor Buggers'.

As the aircraft were based a long way back or at sea, it was decided that two Fleet Arm pilots who were flying Sea Furies from an aircraft carrier should come to 12 (Minden) Battery to experience conditions on the ground. They were not allowed to go forward to the infantry battalions in case of capture. It was a glorious and alcoholic visit and they enjoyed watching the guns spring into action and fire. We would have preferred that they saw a little more action, but when they left they were most appreciative and were clear in their minds that they much preferred flying and returning to the comforts of a carrier rather than sleeping in a dugout. Shaun Jackson was lucky to have the return match and flew in a Fleet Air Arm Avenger aircraft landing on an aircraft carrier, an experience he later described as 'hair raising'. Late-night conversations with the pilots did give an understanding of the significant contribution they were making to the war. I had seen the bombers flying high overhead and heard the exciting swish of the fighters over the OP, but their contribution seemed mainly remote. They talked about the difficulty of finding targets now that the Chinese had learned of the devastating consequences of moving vehicles along roads by day, and how aerial photography had helped them identify lorries and guns which had been hidden in houses with the walls replaced with canvas to avoid detection. There was also discussion about the moral implications of bombing towns and villages. Given that the war on the ground had come to a stalemate, the only strategic offensive initiative left to the United Nations was to bomb, and so Pyongyang and Sinanju had been razed almost to the ground. As the Chinese were hiding weapons in villages it was legitimate to bomb and machine-gun these targets, but the pilots felt uneasy about this as they knew women and children would be killed and injured. It was an unease which manifested itself long after the Korean War, summed up in Vietnam in that emotionally powerful remark: 'I have to destroy your village in order to save your village.' Winston Churchill also felt 'greatly disquieted' about this bombing and after seeing a newsreel of the raid on Pyongyang, on 22 August 1952 he wrote to General Bradley and Field Marshal Alexander saying: 'No one ever thought of splashing napalm about all over the civilian population. I will take no responsibility for it.' The pilots' main concern, however, was the technical superiority the Communists had achieved with their new swept-wing MiG-15 fighter. This Russian-built plane could fly faster, higher, turn more quickly and had better fire power with its 22mm cannons than any United Nations fighter, and had already had a great success against our aircraft. In November 1951 eight 'Superforts' had been attacking an airfield when a clutch of MIG-15s had, in traditional World War Two style, come from 'Six o'clock High – Dead Astern' breaking through the protective fighter screen of Sabres, Meteors and Thunderjets and shooting down three of the bombers and damaging the other five. The Fleet Air Arm pilots were incensed by the ruling that no United Nations aircraft could cross over the Yalu, which meant that the Chinese could build airfields close to the Border and give their fighters the advantage of picking up our aircraft by radar, take off in safety, then position themselves at high altitude ready to dive into the attack. They flew in an area along the Yalu that became known as 'MIG Alley'. This political decision undoubtedly resulted in the deaths and capture of many of our pilots, for if the Chinese pilots were shot down they landed in safe areas while ours landed in enemy territory. The two pilots were robustly ambivalent when asked why the RAF was not taking part in the war. It was one of the paradoxes of the Korean War that the British Government, in its determination not to provoke the Chinese into a major war, was comfortable that HM ships could join the fight and allowed naval pilots to fly Seafire, Sea Furies and Firefly aircraft throughout the war from aircraft carriers, but refused to send RAF fighter aircraft. The pilots knew, however, that a small number of RAF pilots had been clandestinely attached to American and Australian jet-fighter units, and that Flight Lieutenant John Nicholls RAF had been the first United Nations pilot to shoot down a Mig-15. The Government also allowed three squadrons of Sunderland flying boats that were based in Malaya to fly to Japan on a four-week attachment and carry out missions to Korea. They talked about what they called the 'Loch Ness' question, which was the controversial issue as to whether the enemy fighters were being flown by Russian pilots. Voice messages between the enemy fighters and their air controllers had been recorded in Russian, and there was initially a feeling, erroneous as it turned out, that the Chinese were not capable of flying so extremely well in aerial 'dog-fights'. Later, we discovered that Russian pilots *did* fly in 'MIG Alley' and had also trained Chinese pilots who proved as skilful as any in the West. The Communists were able to retain air superiority until the spring of 1953 when the United Nations introduced the American F-86E fighter.

One call sign, which always caused a ripple of excitement both in the command post and on the guns, was call sign 'Six'; this was the Air Op call sign. The Air OP pilots were Royal Artillery officers of 1903 Air Flight who flew little Auster aircraft and were particularly useful in spotting movement and mortar positions on the reverse sides of the Chinese hills. They had flown their Austers from Hong Kong to Korea and initially flew some 5,000 yards behind the enemy front line at heights varying from 3,000 feet to 5,000 feet, but the Chinese got tired of this and brought forward more light anti-aircraft guns and heavy machine guns to knock them down. The fly-line was then cut back considerably. Early one morning, Major Ken Perkins had to fly at 250 feet in order to carry out a photographic mission. He therefore came down out of the sun hoping to find the enemy having breakfast, but as he finished his run there was a loud bang and a single bullet severed both port-side-bearing studs. Luckily, the fuel tank remained intact and he managed to land safely. On another occasion with the Imjin River in full spate (which created great problems as the river could rise forty feet in one night), he had to fly a few feet above the surface to report on a wrecked pontoon bridge. While flying at this low level, his wheels struck some unmarked wires and his aircraft cart-wheeled and plunged into the water. He escaped, but his mechanic drowned. By the ceasefire, Major Perkins had flown 214 sorties, had engaged 470 targets and had been awarded the DFC (Distinguished Flying Cross). Before The Battle of The Hook another Auster aircraft that was trying to get low-level photographic evidence of the Chinese positions was shot down and both the pilot and the observer were killed.

In March 1953 a famous new British battery arrived to join 1 Commonwealth Division, 74 Medium Battery (The Battle Axe Company) RA. This battery was the successor of a company of guns who had been awarded the trophy of a Battle Axe after the capture of Martinique from the French in 1809. The Axe is still with the battery and on 24 February each year is trooped through the ranks carried by the tallest man in the company. As a reminder of the battle the bearer is required to grow a 'full set' of moustaches to represent 'Les Moustaches' from whom the axe was taken.

The requirement for a battery of eight medium 5.5-inch guns was to help in the counter bombardment of the Korean guns and mortars. They were therefore sited in the centre of the divisional area so they could cover the whole front with some overlap onto the neighbouring divisions. After their arrival, the commander Royal Artillery, Brigadier G.P. Gregson DSO, appointed a well-known, albeit sometimes controversial, officer to be the new battery commander. Major Arthur John Batten, always known as 'Jean' Batten had begun the war in 1939 as a Royal Artillery trumpeter. In 1941 while serving in the desert in E Battery R.H.A. he had first been given a MID (Mention in Despatches), was then awarded the DCM (Distinguished Conduct Medal), and finally was promoted to captain in the field. Major Batten was a firm believer that smartness and cleanliness were necessary requisites for good gunnery. Unlike any other battery commander in the division, each Saturday he would inspect the gun lines, the accommodation, the cookhouse, the latrines and, much to the consternation of the gun position officers and troop leaders, the officers' hoochies as well. A shiver of disbelief went around Baker Troop when we heard that officers of 74 Battery had been required to 'Stand by their beds' at awkward times because their hoochie had not been up to standard.

Most of the targets shot by Battle Axe were 'bombards', that is a counter battery targets called for by the Air OP, or were 'flak suppression' targets designed to provide cover when air attacks were being undertaken. Major Batten insisted the guns were manned for the full twenty-four hours and often required one man to be designated who could respond immediately to the call for the DFSOS target by being attached by firing lanyard to a gun. Whereas in Baker Troop we were content to remain in our static position, Major Batten felt that remaining too long in a static position could be detrimental to the ability of the battery if it was required to move quickly. He therefore ordered surprise moves for the whole battery to occupy alternative positions for up to twenty-four periods. He was also very insistent that his battery carried out harassing fire operations and would move one or two guns well forward in order that, under the direction of the air OP, they could engage enemy positions up to a depth of 12,000 yards behind their front line. On 28 March, in support of the Duke of Wellington's on The Hook, the battery fired 150 rounds in forty-five minutes and overall in the battle fired a total of 1181 rounds with a battery response time of fifty seconds. A fine achievement, and Major Batten was subsequently awarded the OBE and his BSM (Battery Sergeant Major), the BEM (British Empire Medal). The Command Post Officer (CPO) of the battery, Captain Mike Everett, was given the Coronation Medal, but when Jean Batten found that the battery was only entitled to six and he had distributed seven, he told Mike Everett to give his back on the basis he was the only officer who had been given one.

It was typical of 'Jean' Batten that when he was required to build an OP in the Front Line, he made, not just a battery OP, but one that became recognised as the 'Divisional OP' and the best place in the whole divisional area for observation. Digging started on the reverse slope of a reserve company location and a large hole was made which was revetted and roofed. Observation over the whole Divisional Front was made possible from a narrow slit in front, which made it the ideal spot to show visiting senior commanders and dignitaries the Chinese Front Line. Although the amount of top cover made it secure inside the OP, the approach was still visible to the enemy and any sign of movement quickly brought a response from the Chinese mortars.

There was a canvas screen running alongside the sunken road behind the OP to prevent the Chinese viewing the road, but at some stage part of this netting had been torn away and there was a subconscious increase of speed as people passed this spot. It became known as 'The Dash' and was watched intently by the Chinese. On 15 July 1953, Lieutenant Maxwell McFarlane RA and Sergeant J.R. Smith were walking back from the OP along 'The Dash,' but were sadly not dashing. They were spotted by a Chinese gunner who fired two mortar bombs and were both wounded. Maxwell arrived in Pusan on 7 July and was wounded on 15 July. The war ended on 27 July. Maxwell was lucky in that his wound was not serious, but because of the humidity at that time it took a long time to heal and he had to spend two weeks in Kure. His journey to Korea had been different from his predecessors in that instead of travelling four weeks in a troop ship he had flown in an Avro York aircraft, an aeroplane based on the design of the wartime Lancaster, to Singapore and then continued his journey by ship. It was the beginning of the end for travel by troopship. Famous ships, which were so much part of the Korean Veterans experience, gradually faded away – *Empire Ken, Halladale, Orwell, Pride, Fowey, Trooper, Windrush* plus the *Dilwara* and *Dunera* became a nostalgic memory.

Administrative functions continued. Once a fortnight there was a Pay Parade. The paying officer and pay clerk sat behind a table supervised by an NCO. Each soldier marched up to the table, saluted, held out his left hand, received his money, leant forward and signed its receipt in the Imprest Account, took a pace back, saluted, turned about and marched off. The currency we used was called British Army Forces Script (BAFS). One morning a very agitated officer arrived at the Baker command post. His task had been to take the signed Imprest Accounts to Regimental HQ, but he had lost the papers. He was very anxious that the soldiers would sign again for the money they had received. Sergeant Major Wroot had a rather tight expression when he signed, but his face was blank when later he reported that of the forty men in the Troop, surprisingly, over thirty had been absent that day either in the OP or on other duties. It was an expensive loss for the officer concerned.

Discipline and punishment did not feature in daily life, but one gunner, recognised to be the scruffiest in the troop, committed some crime that resulted in twenty-eight days' detention in the Canadian-run Commonwealth Provost Unit Prison in Seoul. Twenty-eight days later he entered the command post immaculately dressed with pressed trousers, shining boots, short haircut and throwing an extremely smart salute. What a change. It became clear that Seoul was not a good place to go. The cells were below ground and had a steel grating in place of a ceiling over which the Military Police would patrol and loudly confirm that the soldier was behaving. There was an apocryphal story that an officer went to see one of his soldiers who had refused to obey orders and had stated forcibly that he would soldier no more. The officer found him in Seoul hanging from a hook on the wall with just his head protruding out of a straight jacket. The Provost NCO explained to the rather distressed officer that Gunner X had thrown his food at the guards and destroyed all his issued uniform and therefore, for his own and the guards safety, he had to be restrained, but as soon as he stopped throwing his food at the guards, of course he would be fed and as soon as he would wear his uniform, of course he would be clothed. What Gunner 'X' had to realise was that 'Hard Man' as he considered himself to be, he could not beat the Army and there must be no precedent for a soldier to find a way out of the Service by disobedience.

As there was no Guard Room and every gunner had an operational role to play, minor misdemeanours were punished by stoppage of pay, but one soldier in 107 Battery achieved great notoriety by suffering the traditional punishment of being chained to the gun wheel. He had drunk too much and was unable to man his gun, thus forcing another gunner to take his place and lose his sleep. There was no escort available to take him back, so the Battery Commander ordered that he be chained overnight to a gun wheel until an escort was available. It was very cold so he was given a good supply of blankets and was released next morning. He diluted the solemnity of the sentence by rattling his chain and barking like a dog whenever his friends passed by.

In the command post there was a wind-up gramophone with a limited supply of 78 rpm records. Gunner Prince, who was our wizard on the Artillery Board and who correctly deserved the credit for Baker Troop's quick response to Fire Orders, had a particular favourite. It was a song of no merit and no melody; it was a girl singing 'Water can kill and water can cure, water can raise the temperature... but water can't quench the fire of love.' After the sixth rendition of this song, there arose a great howl from the gun pits making it clear where Gunner Prince should put his fire and water. The more popular song of the time was 'Good Night Irene' which was played continuously, much to the annoyance of Lieutenant Mike Swindells, 5 DG, by his driver in the nearby hoochie. Two other songs which will be very familiar to Korean Veterans were 'China Nights' with the opening line 'Me, I love my Yo Yo' and 'Working for the Yankee dollar'. We had a visit from an ENSA Concert Party which I think included Ted Ray, Charlie Chester and Carole Carr. They did a good job and were cheered and cheered. When one of the girls pulled up her dress to show her garter the noise must have been heard in Pyongyang.

The radio in the command post could also pick up official USA radio broadcasts. These continually gave moral advice, one of which was 'Good morning. This is Radio Osaka Nagoya. Hope you are having a nice day, but remember, a blob on your knob spells no demob. Keep it in your trousers.' This links with the system of giving every soldier a week's leave in Tokyo called Rest and Recuperation (R and R) My turn came round, and together with a group of other officers, I had an uncomfortable eight-hour flight to Tokyo in a Globe-master aircraft. The reception was magnificent. We were put into a bus and with two police cars in front with flashing lights and wailing sirens led to the Ebisu Officers' Leave Centre, scattering cars, bicycles and pedestrians out of the way. It made us feel very important. At Ebisu I was allocated a room with a subaltern from the Duke of Wellington's Regiment. We got on very well together. For the first time I wore the two medal Korean ribbons on my battledress, and instead of the 40 Divisional Cockerel Patch on my sleeve, wore the Commonwealth Division emblem. The bar was an animated, throbbing room run by the Australians and full of officers of all nationalities all wanting to have a good time. We went shopping in the Ginza where it seemed unbelievable that these quiet, courteous people should be the same people who, only a few years before, had carried out such atrocities. There was no sign of war damage and compared with London the shops were full of luxury items. I bought Noritake china and little Japanese dolls for presents. The most sensible thing to buy were Mikimoto Pearls but the most popular items were kimonos. Some officers who went to Kure for their R and R took taxis to Hiroshima and Nagasaki and were surprised how quickly these two cities had been rebuilt. At that time the word 'radiation' was never mentioned, neither were the possible residual radioactive dangers of the atomic bomb ever discussed. We went to a well-known dance hall on the fourth floor of the Maranouchi Hotel which was full of a colourful variety of officers from the Commonwealth, drank Asahi beer and were joined by beautifully-delicate Japanese girls. They sat down and prettily asked if we would buy them a drink – a fizzy-coloured concoction in a shallow champagne glass – and they then agreed to dance. No money changed hands, but it was clear that the more often their glass was filled the better the dancing would become. After months living in the dugouts it was a very pleasant interlude. In the plane on the way back my Duke's friend and I agreed R and R was indeed a recuperating experience but not a restful one.

CHAPTER SIX

The Hook Battles

Back in the routine of OP tours and gun position duties, everyone became aware of the tense situation developing on a feature known as 'The Hook'. The Hook was a hill that protruded out from our line of defence and thrust into the Chinese front line. The frustrating and intermittent ceasefire talks continued at Panmunjom, and before the talks were concluded, it was clear that the Chinese wanted this hill to be under their control when the fighting stopped.

It was a situation reminiscent of the First World War when the Ypres Salient and Hill 60 protruded into the German Front Line and became the scene of bitter fighting. Although only a low feature of some 200 metres high it dominated the Samichon Valley and from the top, observation was possible over the two vital crossing points across the Imjin River that carried the main routes to the east. If it fell into enemy hands, the whole of the west sector of the UN Front would be threatened and, as the next suitable ground for a defensive line was more than five miles south of the Imjin, its capture by the Chinese would be very serious.

In March 1952 when the Canadian 1 Battalion Princess Patricia's Canadian Light Infantry occupied The Hook, the Chinese launched a savage attack but suffered severe casualties and had been repulsed. In October 1952, when the American Marines occupied the position, the Chinese tried again and this time managed to push the Marines off the forward positions. A daylight counter-attack was organised, and following an intense air and artillery bombardment, the Marines were successful and the Chinese ejected. On 3/4 November, the Black Watch relieved the Marines whose Colonel told them that he had fought the Japanese throughout the Pacific War and had never encountered such fierce opposition. He predicted that the Black Watch would be able to stay on The Hook for a maximum of twenty-four hours. At 2100hrs on the night 18/19 November after a heavy daylight bombardment, a Chinese force, estimated at battalion strength, tried again. Two companies of the Black Watch, plus two platoons, fought through the night, and although the battalion received between 4,000 to 5,000 rounds of mortar and artillery shells, the Scotsmen held their ground. The fighting eventually stopping at 0630 hrs.

In May 1953, when the Commonwealth Division returned to the line, the Chinese again decided that The Hook must be captured and began moving artillery and infantry forward in preparation for a major attack. At this time the Black Watch was back on The Hook, the King's Regiment was on the feature to their right called Yong Dong and the Duke of Wellington's Regiment was in reserve. In preparation for this major attack, on the night 7/8 May the Chinese launched a company strength probing against the Black Watch. The Chinese attacked with determination, and some, carrying coconut matting as a makeshift bridging, managed to cross the barbed wire in front of the forward platoons. They were halted by a concentration of fire from the Battalion support weapons and the artillery, but mainly by the courage of the soldiers who stayed and fought. The gunner OP officer who was attached to the Black Watch said: 'It was a battalion that oozed efficiency.' Lieutenant Donald McNab, who commanded a platoon and was twice wounded, had little time for the issued 7-inch-round bayonet, which looked like a nail: 'It was a wee pointed thing that was only useful for punching holes in carnation milk tins.' So he bought his platoon heavy 9-inch sheath knives from Japan. The weapons of his platoon were still the 303 bolt-action rifle, the Sten gun, Bren gun and 2-inch mortar. Only when going on patrol were the soldiers issued with the heavy green flak vest, which was made from manganese plates sewn into a waistcoat of ballistic nylon; so very different from the current issue which is light and made from layers of woven-laminated fibres. One night Donald McNab took out a Fighting Patrol accompanied by a Royal Engineer NCO with a dog. The dog was trained not to bark, but if he smelled a Chinese soldier he was to growl. There was a lot of growling but no Chinese and the experiment was not repeated.

A great asset to every unit in the Division was the constant supply of aerial photos. Every morning photographic sorties were flown along the whole Divisional Front from The Hook position on the left to Hill 365 on the right. Officers from the Intelligence Corps 104 Army Photographic Interpretation Section (104) APIS did an immediate print scrutiny to a depth of two miles, and by comparing previous traces were immediately able to pinpoint new trenches, caves, gun positions and vehicle tracks. A secondary in-depth review would then take place covering the rear areas. General West would insist on an APIS briefing every morning following his normal morning prayers, and, when attacks were expected, Captain Hamish Eaton, Intelligence Corps commanding the APIS, would take the photos and traces directly to the relevant battalion or company, which enabled the company commanders to see the reverse slopes of the Chinese hills directly to their front. In Baker Troop OP we pinned detailed photos on the wall of the Chinese opposite, especially marking the caves housing their self-propelled 76mm guns, which we disliked intensely. These small caves were dug deep underground with an access on the reverse slope; they were often unoccupied as one gun would have several alternative positions. Neither the 25-pdr guns nor the mortars were very successful in destroying these gun slits, but 1 RTR Centurion tanks with direct fire had more success. By the end of the War, the Chinese had demonstrated a remarkable ability for digging; forward positions were often four storeys deep and, if they were attacked at ground level, they were able to move down and down and then re-emerge at a different location. Communication trenches were dug deep and could run, out of sight, for ten miles behind the Front Line giving considerable cover from air attack and the ability to concentrate for a surprise attack.

Throughout this Hook Battle, Baker Troop had been fully committed, 12 (Minden) Battery remained in direct support of the King's Regiment, and most of our fire orders had been relayed from the 107 Battery OP which was in direct support of the Black Watch. More and more of these fire orders requested Variable Time (VT) air-burst shells. Experience had shown that the Chinese were most vulnerable in the period after they had left their dugouts and were racing across the ground to our wire defences. The VT shells burst above the ground spraying fragments from above and had a devastating effect on troops in the open. The shells, we were told, were very expensive and it took time to set the fuses, but checking the wounds on the dead Chinese proved their value.

We were all aware that the Chinese were planning another major attack on The Hook; the big question was when. Large quantities of reserve shells and cartridges arrived at the troop position; so much that the No. 1's had to stack it unprotected outside, but close to the gun pits. This was a procedure they disliked intensely, given the obvious danger of an explosion. I continued completing OP tours with the King's Regiment on Yong Dong, and compared the situation to a gambler who was watching the roulette ball go round and round waiting for it to finally stop. I knew the attack would come but would the ball land on the date when I was in the OP or at the gun position?

About this time, in order to strengthen the artillery support available for the coming battle, a battery of 25-pdr guns from 16 New Zealand Field Artillery Regiment was attached to our regiment. They were very fast, so fast in reporting 'READY', that the suspicion grew that they were being economical with the truth and were reporting 'ready' before it was true. As an act of courtesy, therefore, and to see the Kiwis in action, two of us drove over one afternoon to pay our respects. The 16 New Zealand Field Regiment was a remarkably successful and very professional gunner regiment which earned the respect and appreciation of every infantry battalion it supported. On its formation in 1950, it had only four regular officers and one regular NCO; all the other members were volunteers. After three months' training, the battery arrived in Pusan in December 1950, and had then taken part in every major action. Their gun drill may have made a Larkhill gunnery instructor wriggle a little, but we observed a shoot and they were genuinely first and accurate. In the evening we were asked to stay for a meal and a drink so, as was the prudent custom at the time, we removed the rotor arm from the jeep and accepted their Kiwi liquid hospitality. Much later, when it was time to return, we replaced the rotor arm and set off through the night over the paddy fields. It was pitch black with no moon or stars, and as we were near to the Front Line, we could only use our sidelights. It was so difficult to see ahead that my friend leaned out of the door on his side and I leaned out on my side trying to pick up the edge of the track. Suddenly, out of the darkness, an American policeman wearing the traditional white helmet stopped us and asked for identification. When reassured we were a couple of 'Brits' he waved us on and then politely said: 'Excuse me Sir, would it not be easier if you lowered your bonnet?'

Every night now Chinese shelling increased, and on the night of 20/21 May over 4,000 rounds fell mainly on The Hook position. Many senior officers, including the divisional commander General Cassels, who had commanded the famous 51st Highland Division in the European Campaign, stated that this weight of enemy artillery fire had never been experienced in the Second World War on any front. Brigadier Kendrew decided, therefore, to readjust his forces; The Duke of Wellington Regiment was put back on The Hook, with the Black Watch just behind, sited for immediate counter-attack on either The Hook Left Sector or The Hook Right Sector and the King's Regiment was deployed on the right. It was interesting that among the captured Chinese weapons were British Bren Guns manufactured in 1942, and ammunition dated 1943, which had almost certainly been carried by the transport planes which flew that hazardous, and often fatal, journey over the 'The Hump' to supply the Nationalist Army of General Chiang Kai Shek.

In this period of waiting, the Brigadier decided to mount a diversionary attack to the right of The Hook using B Company of 1 King's. The Company moved out on the night 24/25 May down to the Samichon River. A firm base was established just beyond our defensive minefield, and one platoon, heavily armed with additional Bren guns, moved down to the river to form an advanced base. A second platoon led by Captain John Caws was lightly armed with sten guns and grenades, and crossed the River to attack the Chinese positions and try to capture a prisoner. Baker Troop was firing continuously on targets just above the attacking platoon. Unfortunately, Captain Caws ran into an unmarked minefield and the noise attracted Chinese fire. Out of his sixteen men, ten were injured, four of whom were stretcher casualties. Captain Caws was among the wounded and three weeks later we were in adjoining hospital beds.

Then, one morning, an unprecedented event occurred. Colonel Brennan arrived at the battery position and summoned all ranks to gather round him. He stood next to Baker One and said that there was positive intelligence that a Chinese attack on The Hook was imminent. He said it would be hard battle and that we should be prepared, but he was confident we could defeat the attack. It was a good speech and left everyone with a sense of determination, although a little apprehensive. The intelligence that convinced the colonel that the attack was imminent came from that most reliable of sources, a man who knew the facts. As in Northern Ireland, although photographic intelligence, forensic intelligence, card indexes, and reports from units all help guess future operations, nothing beats a human source who has access to those who are actually planning and going to implement operations. This is why source handling became so important and remains so today. In this case, a Chinese private soldier called Private Hua Hong, who had previously fought for Chiang Kai Shek and had then been conscripted into the People's Revolutionary Army, walked into our front line and surrendered. He confirmed that an attack was being planned and that he had taken part in a specific rehearsal on a hill similar to The Hook ten miles back from the front. The attacking force would consist of five assault companies from the 397th, 398th and 399th Regiments carrying satchel charges to cut the wire, destroy our gun pits and command posts, and were to be followed by three other fighting companies from the 399th Regiment. Just as the area of The Hook meant that only one company could be used to defend the position, so the Chinese were limited in the number of men they could use in the initial attack. Their aim was to kill the defenders, seize the ground and then bring up reserves. Hua Hong knew a great deal but did not know the exact date for the attack.

His unexpected arrival in the Black Watch lines caused a flurry of excitement. The Commonwealth Divisional policy was to give a bottle of whisky and five days' leave in Japan for any soldier who captured a prisoner. This followed a tradition established in World War One. When Hong was pulled to the ground and made prisoner, his captors naturally expected the promised rewards. Sadly, the fact that he had been a voluntary prisoner, but more especially because this was not a good time to let two soldiers disappear to Tokyo, meant the rewards were not forthcoming. Another incident which also failed to bring a reward was when a soldier discovered and arrested a Chinese soldier on the flank of his company position, only to be told he had successfully captured one of the Korean labourers who, on the Battalion's behalf, was digging a communication trench.

Signals Intelligence, which by 1953 had been refined and properly targeted, was working well and also indicated an imminent attack. An attack was coming – but when? The answer came at 1935 hrs exactly on 28 May; with all four companies of the Duke of Wellington's Regiment deployed on The Hook, and a further company of the King's in reserve, the battle started. It was still daylight and fighting opened with a tremendous artillery barrage falling on The Hook and surrounding positions. The Chinese, who had been lying concealed in caves close to our forward platoons, advanced aggressively behind their artillery barrage led by their assault engineers carrying satchel charges to clear a path through our barbed wire. They quickly crossed the protective minefields and wire obstacles and within minutes were attacking the forward weapon pits.

On the afternoon of 28 May, Major Mackay, commanding 45 Battery, had decided to increase the number of OPs in support of Captain John Gordon, the gunner OP officer with the Duke's forward company, and asked Lieutenant Roddy Scott, the OP officer with C Company 1 DWR on a feature to the right known as 'The Sausage', to send two of his gunners over to The Hook to man an additional observation post. Roddy sent Bombardier H.J. Hudson and Gunner M.L.Caws who, on arrival on The Hook, moved to an OP with the forward company in 10 Platoon area and, during the period of intense shelling before the assault of the Chinese, began to relay fire orders back to Captain Gordon using their 31 radio set. After the Chinese assault succeeded in crossing the wire and ran screaming down the trenches carrying satchel charges and using their burp guns and hand grenades, the two men carried on reporting the enemy movements for eight minutes and, according to Captain Gordon, 'behaved with coolness and determination.' Surrounded by the enemy, 10 Platoon commander ordered VT artillery fire down on his own position but was then killed. Gunner Caws came on the air and reported that the

Chinese were all around him, but his transmission suddenly ceased and his body, together with that of Bombardier Hudson, was found next day beside the wrecked radio. They had been killed by a satchel charge thrown into the back of their OP. They had died with their infantry comrades doing their gunner duty. Four other gunners from 45 Battery with the Duke's were also wounded that night.

In December 1953, Major R. E. Austin, who had been a King's officer in the Second World War, and was then a company commander with the Duke of Wellington's Regiment, was asked to write an official account of the battle for the *Journal of the King's Regiment*:

> Within a matter of minutes, the platoon commander was killed in hand-to-hand fighting and the Chinese overran the platoon, leaving behind them small pockets of resistance and many of our men buried in the debris. While this fighting was taking place, three additional waves of enemy, each of approximately platoon strength, swept forward. They were practically annihilated by our artillery fire and few were able to join those already precariously holding on to the top of The Hook. These, however, reorganised and attempted an encircling movement the right arm of which was caught in the wire on top of The Hook and was wiped out by artillery and small arms fire. The time was now close to 2030 hrs when the Chinese artillery fire lifted to the road behind The Hook along the road that reinforcements would have to travel.
>
> On top of The Hook there was an uneasy lull which was broken at 2045 hrs when a fresh Chinese attack came in. Although this attack was savaged by artillery, tank and LMG (light machine-gun) fire, the enemy succeeded in linking up with their force, which had penetrated our right-hand platoon and fierce hand-to-hand fighting broke out. Greater penetration was achieved until most of our platoon area was in enemy hands. The platoon was reinforced and the penetration was held. Subsequently a planned counter-attack restored the situation.
>
> At 2305 hrs the CO ordered heavy artillery, tank and MMG

(medium machine-gun) fire to be brought down on what looked like the forming-up place for an attack and no attack materialised. It was later confirmed that this enemy force was of battalion strength and was caught by artillery in the open and suffered enormous casualties – so much so that it advanced but a short distance from its start line and was then forced to clear the battlefield of dead and wounded.

The final attack came in at 0030hrs, this time directed at The Hook. It was of company strength and was heavily engaged by the tanks and the MMGs of the King's and Duke's with artillery and mortar support. Slowly and methodically the area was cleared and by 0330 hrs The Hook was reported completely in our hands.

The scene of devastation that was unfolded in the grey dawn that followed was indescribable. Bunkers were smashed to matchwood, communication trenches that the night before had been six to eight feet deep were now scarcely knee high. Shredded sandbags and smashed pieces of barbed wire littered the area and dead Chinese, many in fragments from the murderous effect of our artillery fire, rounded off a scene that rivalled the most gruesome illustrations in Dante's inferno.

Captain Tony Harris, now commanding Baker Troop, relieved Captain Gordon and was forced to use an open trench for observation as the OP had been destroyed. On the next day I went up to The Hook which was now occupied by 1st Battalion Royal Fusiliers. My first impression was that everyone was dazed. Soldiers were scrambling along the blown-in trenches and trying to dig out the weapon pits and command posts. It was rather like the scene after an earthquake where everybody is trying to regain normality. It had been a terrifying night, one that would have been very familiar to infantrymen in the First World War. screaming enemy getting through the defensive minefield; crossing the barbed wire and then jumping into the zigzag communication trenches behind the weapon pits. It became a personal battle of Sten gun, revolver, grenade and bayonet versus Chinese stick grenades and 'Burp' guns, all against the overpowering backdrop noise of the Chinese mortars and artillery and the British machine gun, tank and artillery fire. The Chinese had desperately wanted to capture this hill and the Duke's prevented it happening. As I walked through the position my feelings can be summed up in two words – 'admiration' and 'respect'. This was the feeling I had at the time and on subsequent analysis, this feeling of admiration and respect has increased. The officers, the warrant officers, the NCOs, and above all, the young National Servicemen, were put to the ultimate test and by determination and bravery were successful. Sixteen infantry battalions served in Korea during the war and, as is traditional, every battalion finds it easy to highlight the failings of other battalions. I never met any soldier who knew the facts, who would not agree that the 1st Battalion the Duke of Wellington's Regiment supported by the 1st Battalion King's Regiment justifiably deserved the praise and decorations they received for their actions on the night of 28 May 1953. For those who do not know the facts the book by A.J. Barker *Fortune favours the Brave* is a wonderful account of this most dramatic battle.

Major Austin in his factual report continually mentions the effect on the battle of the artillery and mortar fire that supplemented the fire from the troop of 1 RTR located on The Hook itself. The fact that so much artillery fire was able to be concentrated on such a small area at the right time was the result of a well-planned and professional artillery plan. Major Bill MacKay and Captain Gordon had prepared the Defensive Fire Plan and had registered targets covering the area leading up to The Hook, targets immediately in front of the barbed wire, targets actually on the forward platoons and targets inside the battalion perimeter. Not surprisingly, Captain Gordon was awarded an 'Immediate MC' for his actions during the Battle and his citation reads: 'Throughout the night his cool and balanced situation reports and his efficient calls for fire were of the utmost value in helping first to stop the enemy and then to defeat and drive him from the position. There is no doubt that the correct deployment of the guns had a major effect on the outcome of the Battle. Captain Gordon's contribution to this was notable. In the words of the company commander, he was a tower of strength.'

It is a wonderful citation describing a gunner officer fulfilling his role.

Throughout the battle, Major MacKay, the battery commander, sat next to the Duke's battalion commander, Colonel Bunbury, relaying requests for fire back to Colonel Brennan. Colonel Brennan was given the authority to coordinate the fire from the guns of 1 Regiment Royal Canadian Artillery, 16 Field Regiment Royal New Zealand Artillery and the mortars of 61 Light Regiment. Brigadier Gregson, the commander Royal Artillery, at Divisional Headquarters coordinated the guns of 74 (Battle Axe Company) RA and all the medium and heavy guns from the flank divisions that were in range. A total of 25,743 rounds were fired that night, mainly on The Hook position and Baker Troop played its part.

Starting around 1700 hrs Baker Troop was called into action firing on targets where the Chinese might be forming up and then, as the tempo of battle developed, gradually increased their firing rate. Given the desperate situation of the Duke's, there is some guilt in reporting that the feeling in the Troop was one of exultation. Members of gun teams had to stand around for long periods in all types of weather and often did not fire; if they did it was generally, at most, three rounds' gunfire. On the night of 28 May, the orders came and came, 'Five rounds Gunfire! Five rounds Gunfire', then the most unusual order, 'Repeat' and again, 'Repeat.' There was an air of feverish activity as rounds were thrust into the breech, rammed home and the gun fired. Every soldier in the Troop, signallers, mechanics, cooks and batmen, clustered around the gun pits helping carry the shells, empty the ammunition boxes and remove the spent cartridge cases. We fired every type of shell we possessed, variable time fuse (VT), High Explosive, Smoke and shells that were designed to carry propaganda leaflets.

At one stage, a convoy of lorries arrived driven by RASC drivers commanded by Lieutenant David Lawrence who had been in the same intake at Sandhurst. He and the drivers unloaded their wagons and carried the ammunition directly to the guns. Given the rate of fire, the muzzle of Baker Four was glowing red in the darkness and Lieutenant Lawrence ran back to his wagon, took out his towel, soaked it in cold water and threw it over the barrel where it burst into flames. At daylight, when the battle on The Hook was drawing to an end, the Chinese made a fresh attack on the Turkish Brigade to our left and the Troop was again called into action. This fire was successfully coordinated – in spite of language problems – by Second Lieutenant W.J. Bromley, who was the survey officer of 20th Field Regt, but who had been attached as liaison officer to the Turkish Brigade for this purpose.

During the night 20th Field Regiment fired 13,609 rounds and Baker Troop nearly 2,000. Looking down from the command post next morning, the piles of empty ammunition boxes were an unforgettable sight. That morning more ammunition arrived, and we felt a warm sense of gratitude to all those in the RAOC who had made the supreme effort to move such large quantities of ammunition forward, and to the RASC drivers who had got it to our guns including, we were told, the enthusiastic but rather bewildered driver of the mobile bath and laundry truck. When Lieutenant Lawrence visited us later we made him an Honorary Member of Baker Troop and presented him with a bottle of sherry and a new towel.

At 1700 hrs on 28 May, 248 Battery 61 Light Regiment RA who were supporting 28 Brigade on the right flank of the Division, were suddenly ordered to move to the other end of the Divisional area and give support to the Duke's. As the battle had already started, they deployed off the line of march and immediately started engaging targets. They continued until the mortar barrels glowed red with heat. At one stage, Second Lieutenant Peter Duffield, the troop commander of G Troop, was given the order, 'Gunfire 10 Seconds', which meant he should fire one round of mortar bombs every ten seconds. When he queried how many rounds, he was told by his OP officer to continue firing until told to stop, a most unusual order. He also remembers that throughout the night more bombs were delivered in wagons driven by the Transport Company of the Royal Canadian Army Service Corps. On 28 May, the three mortar troops fired an amazing total of 8,000 bombs. Usually the mortars DFs were about 500 yards from our front line, but in The Hook battle this was reduced to 200 yards. The gunner mortars had earned the gratitude of the infantry, but were also treated with a little apprehension as the Number 9 tail fin of the bomb had a tendency to fracture and come off which caused the bomb to fall only 40 yards in front of the mortar. Second Lieutenant Duffield can remember this happening and watching a gunner run forward and, to the amazement of the infantry, pick up the bomb and run back with it under his arm to his gun pit. Sometimes the infantry reference to the gunners as 'Drop Shorts' was justified. On 14 July 1953, 61 Light Regiment celebrated firing its 250,000th bomb, having been in front line action more than any other gunner regiment.

The tanks of 1 RTR also played an important part in the battle. In the days proceeding 28 May, Captain George Forty, in consultation with the company commanders of the Duke's, had pre-selected a large number of targets, given them a number and registered the angle of traverse and elevation. Unfortunately, just before the battle, Captain Forty was badly wounded by a mortar bomb as he got out of his tank to initiate a direct fire shoot. In his place Lieutenant Tony Uloth, who had previously been on The Hook, was suddenly recalled to take over. By 1730 hrs on 28 May when the Chinese artillery fire was reaching a crescendo, Lieutenant Uloth moved his four tanks up to their peg markers and with their hatches closed awaited the enemy attack. At about 1830 hrs a high-explosive shell hit his tank with a sound like a very large sledgehammer and a shower of sparks came through the machine gun mounting. Twice more during the night his tank was hit but, although this was very alarming, he was able to continue firing both his 20-pounder and machine gun. At 1945 hrs he received the message from the company commander, 'Enemy attack imminent' and then a call for fire on his own position. This was a target that had been previously taken into account by Colonel David Rose, commanding officer of the Black Watch who, when taking over from the US Marines, had made an urgent request for a troop of sappers and one hundred Korean labourers to dig very deep gun pits, command posts and communication trenches, some over eight feet in depth. He had anticipated that in the event of the Chinese infantry getting through the wire and on to his forward position, his soldiers could go into their deep holes and leave the Chinese exposed on the roofs. This very dangerous artillery fire plan had the appropriate codename 'Tin-Hat'. For the tanks it was a target that had not been registered, but working from his map Lieutenant Uloth was able to adjust his fire to the forward edge of The Hook, which they then swept through the night with continuous machine gun fire and explosive shells.

As an aid to accurate shooting, tanks were fitted with high-powered searchlights. The problem was that when a tank fired, it created so much smoke and dust that the light was of little value. The answer was to move a second tank with a searchlight close to the firing tank which gave the firing tank light and better vision. This tactic was used in the battle but, perhaps not surprisingly, the searchlight was soon hit and put out of action. Other troops of the regiment sited on the flanks were also able to provide direct fire on the attacking Chinese, and by the morning the Squadron had fired 504 rounds of high explosive and 22,500 machine gun rounds. The only damage to Lieutenant Uloth's tank was that all the turret bins had been blown away and the searchlight badly damaged. The Centurion tank had proved itself in battle, and thereafter there was no complaint from the soldiers about the noise of the tanks.

CHAPTER SEVEN

The Attack on the Warsaw Caves

The war then became very personal. During their various attacks on The Hook, the Chinese had tried to reduce their casualties by digging caves ever closer and closer to our Front Line, and so shortening the distance after crossing their Start Lines before reaching our wire. There was now photographic evidence that they were doing the same thing again and getting much closer to The Hook on a feature known as 'Warsaw'. The caves were dug on their reverse slopes and so avoided our artillery and mortar fire. Brigadier Kendrew decided, therefore, that they should be destroyed and the unit to do it would be Charlie Company, 1st Battalion King's Regiment.

On 1 June I had a call from Johnnie King-Martin to go to 1 King's and report for a briefing to Major McL. 'Dinky' Dynes commanding Charlie Company. Major Dynes was an experienced officer who had been commissioned into The King's Regiment in 1938 and had fought with the 2nd Battalion at the bloody Battle of Cassino where his commanding officer and sixty Kingsmen had been killed. Major Dynes' plan was as follows; Charlie Company, with a detachment from 55 Field Squadron RE with one officer, Captain G.L. Cooper and fourteen men plus myself as Forward Observation Officer (FOO), were to mount a company night attack, move out from The Hook, follow the line of the Samichon River, reach the caves and blow them up. There were a total of fifteen caves in three re-entrants known as 'Rip', 'Van', and 'Winkle'. A firm base consisting of the Company HQ and one platoon was to be established on a knoll called 'Doughnut', then three fighting patrols were to go forward to attack each re-entrant. Major

Dynes told me that my job was 'to stick to him like glue.' The photos supplied by 104 APIS were invaluable in planning our route as it was dominated on both sides by hills held by the Chinese. I carried an annotated print with me during the attack.

The next day, 2 June, was Coronation Day and it was decided that the whole divisional artillery would fire a 'Feu de Joie' from left to right with concentrations of red, white and blue smoke. Baker Troop fired white smoke, although subsequently there was an allegation that instead of all-white smoke, one Gun Number One had included white phosphorous. In the afternoon I went back to the Yong Dong position to make a Fire Plan. A Black Watch corporal guided me to a good forward site and I plotted and registered a series of targets on either side of the caves and on the hill above the caves. While doing this I was joined by Captain Dick Trant who was doing the same thing for the medium guns of 74 (Battle Axe Company). After plotting the Fire Plan we were both invited to share the hospitality of the Black Watch as they celebrated the Coronation in traditional Scottish style with a large glass of whisky and three cheers for Her Majesty.

Captain George Cooper was also preparing for his role in the attack, and decided that as it meant carrying explosive through some 4000 yards of hostile territory, his sappers would each carry twenty pounds of explosive in lightweight haversacks and a Sten gun. On reaching the caves they would place a small tamping charge at each entrance linked by cortex cord to two 8lb charges with a thirty second delay initiation. It was a good plan as the tunnels would probably be shallow, and if a bigger charge were used the blast would tend to blow straight out of the tunnel and cause little damage. Events showed that it was the right decision and the tunnels were shallow.

I selected two gunners to go with me, Lake and Cassidy. I had a microphone and headset and Gunner Lake carried the 31 wireless with an extension link to me. Gunner Cassidy carried the spare batteries. We borrowed three flak vests from the BQMS.

At 2200 hrs on 4 June we moved down from The Hook following a route that had been cleared earlier by the Assault Pioneers. It was dark with no stars. Knowing that there were a great number of mines scattered over the Samichon Valley, we moved as quietly as possible in single file along an ill-defined and overgrown path. Suddenly there was a noise from the flank and I drew my revolver feeling very vulnerable. It was quite a relief when a deer scampered past the Company Commander. A little later, a King's man stepped on a jumping mine which detonated, killing three soldiers next to me and wounding eleven others. As I lay on the ground, my first thought was, 'Well it has happened but I am all right.' I could feel wetness on my left leg but nothing serious. After checking that Gunner Lake was OK we moved back to join the company commander.

The casualties disrupted the original plan to have three assaulting teams, so the company commander very sensibly decided to concentrate all his force and attack only the main re-entrant – 'Rip'. I asked him whether I should join this attacking group but was told to stay where I was. With the noise of grenades and the mine explosion, the Chinese were now well aware something was happening and fire came down from our flanks. I pulled out my Fire Plan, and then discovered I had not brought a torch! Luckily, very luckily, I had memorised the Target Numbers and began calling for fire. Gunner Lake was having difficulty getting through on his set, and so I was most grateful to use the Sapper link which, with traditional Sapper reliability, became the main means of communication throughout the night. We later discovered that a large piece of the metal had passed through the 31 Set Gunner Lake had on his back and had lodged at the base of his spine in his flak vest. This was why we could not get through on our set.

As the attack group advanced, I gradually moved the fire targets towards the top of the 'Rip' re-entrant, and on a signal from the company commander that the assault party was in position, moved the targets to the rear. Second Lieutenant Williams led the assault and reached the caves, which were about 100 yards up the re-entrant. They threw grenades into this first cave but at the second were met by 'Burp' gun fired at point-blank range, followed by a grenade. Lieutenant Williams climbed on top of this cave and killed the occupants with his hand grenades. In Major Austin's account of this attack he states:

> By this time the enemy had been alerted and the re-entrant was humming like a disturbed hornets nest. The Chinese were

firing automatic weapons and rolling grenades down the steep sides. Many of the raiding party were wounded and soon only the commander and three men including one sapper were left unwounded. Lieutenant Williams decided to withdraw and ordered all but the sapper and himself to help the wounded. The sapper blew up the cave and Lieutenant Williams remained behind to help another badly-wounded sapper. He got the wounded sapper back to the FUP but it was under mortar fire so he decided to lie up in the paddy with the sapper and get him back when the opportunity presented itself. Fortunately, Lieutenant Cross took a small rescue party back to find him and escorted them both safely back.'

Throughout all this period, I was with the company commander passing fire orders to the guns. I later leaned that Johnnie King-Martin had made exceptional efforts to provide cover and had arranged for the divisional artillery to fire continuously on the enemy positions overlooking our position in the valley. At 0415 hrs the order was given to withdraw, and Gunner Lake and I carried a stretcher back. We had lost three soldiers and twenty-seven were wounded, including me.

Included in the plan of the attack was the availability of armour. Lieutenant Uloth was selected for this role and, as it meant driving up the narrow path with paddy on either side, he decided to lead with only one tank but prudently had a second tank close behind. He fitted both tanks with tow ropes to make a hook-up if the need arose. His plan worked, he reached the area of the caves and provided covering fire throughout the night. Then, feeling rather vulnerable sitting in the middle of the valley, he pulled back with the withdrawing infantry. Enemy fire was following us and so more tanks were deployed into the valley and provided direct fire support.

At 0500 hrs we reached The Hook where Freddy Newall welcomed me and helped me to the Regimental Aid Post (RAP). Here our Regimental Medical Officer, Dr. Keith Glennie Smith, cleaned my wounds, gave me antibiotics, a shot of morphine from a sachet which looked like a toothpaste tube with a needle, and applied a shell dressing. After this, I only have a vague memory of a bumpy journey on a stretcher in the back of a jeep with three other casualties and then waking up in a hospital ward.

The conclusion of the raid by Captain George Cooper, later General Sir George Cooper KCB, MC, was: 'This raid, though not successful in destroying all the Chinese tunnels, resulted in heavy casualties to the enemy and their abandonment of their re-entrants in the valley for fear of being attacked in the rear. It also resulted in no further attacks being made on The Hook.' The CO of the King's wrote to our CO that the 'Artillery support had been magnificent,' but the most satisfying part was in hospital when Lieutenant Williams came to see me and said that if it had not been for the artillery fire hitting the top of the re-entrant during the assault, they would all have been killed. He was awarded an immediate MC and Lieutenant R.A. Cross and Lieutenant Uloth were awarded a Mention in Dispatches.

On 6 June, the day after the raid, Shaun Jackson wrote a letter to his mother and father saying: 'Polly went out on a company raid as a forward observation officer the other day and apparently did very well. He got slightly wounded with a bullet in the behind and a bit of mine in his thigh and will be in hospital for about three weeks.'

CHAPTER EIGHT

The Last Fighting Phase for Baker Troop

T he hospital was in Uijongbu, about twelve miles north of Seoul, and was called the 'NORMASH', a Norwegian-run Mobile Army Surgical Hospital. Although it was not an American MASH as depicted in the wonderful TV programme, it had a very similar atmosphere. The surgeons and doctors were excellent, as were the nurses. However, as the nurses were all male I missed the opportunity of meeting a Norwegian equivalent of 'Hot Lips'. The following morning after arrival, I was visited by the excellent Dr. Glennie Smith who said the surgery was to take place that afternoon and asked if I minded him carrying out the operation. This was agreed and he successfully took out bits, sowed up bits and left some bits in as being too small to warrant cutting them out. Over the past fifty years these little bits have gradually worked their way out and when this happens I am always jolted back from the seemingly important, but transient problems of the moment, to remember those who were standing next to me on the night of 4 June are now resting in the cemetery in Pusan.

The hospital ward was a jolly place. In the bed on my right was a Canadian who, when restless at night, sang 'Hill Billy' songs. On my right was Captain John Caws who became a great friend, but who sadly died in a motorcycle accident some years later. Opposite me was a Duke's officer who had been remarkably lucky; a piece of metal had entered his cheek, passed through his mouth and out the other side without damaging teeth or jaw. Recovery was fairly quick, and after about ten days I got out of bed for the first time and went to the cinema. This was the afternoon that Shaun came to see his wounded friend and was very amused that I had gone to the pictures. He ensured that this story spread round the regiment and was retold for many years, totally destroying my image as a wounded hero.

I had a couple of days in the General Hospital in Seoul and then went to a convalescent unit by the sea. This again was a jolly experience; there were several Duke's officers there including David Gilbert Smith, the great rugby player who won an MC for leading a counter attack on the night of The Hook Battle, and there was much laughter and banter. There was also a wind-up gramophone with one record that I played again and again. It still remains a most evocative piece, Mozart's *Clarinet Concerto*.

I arrived back in Baker Troop on 29 June and Lieutenant Alan Woodford arrived on 30 June. As a new gun position office, I was sent back up to the Baker Troop OP. The King's Regiment was on Yong Dong and I lived with B Company commanded by Major Gordon Beard in the platoon area commanded by Lieutenant Mervyn Ryder. His platoon had a catch phrase that was repeated endlessly.

Soldier 1: 'Do you come from Liverpool?'
Soldier 2: 'No, I come from Birkenhead'
Everybody: 'But from our house you can see the Liver Buildings!'

One sunny morning, while peacefully minding my own business in the OP dugout, there was a swishing, whistling sound, followed by a savage cracking sound as a shell burst just to the right of the OP slit. A minute later a second shell hit the roof of the OP and destroyed the aerial, then a third shell smacked to the left of the OP. It was quite clear that someone with a self-propelled 76mm gun was specifically trying to knock out Baker Troop OP. The phone rang and it was a call from our forward platoon asking why we were digging. A few days earlier, mortar fire had destroyed the communication trench between the OP and the troop command post, and I had requested help from the gun line to clear the debris. These gunners had arrived and were doing the digging, but they were throwing the soil over the parapet and this was clearly seen from the forward platoon, and, evidently, by a Chinese gunner on the other side of the valley. He thought three rounds of 76mm direct fire would be a good thing to do. While crouching on the floor of the OP, Gunner John Page next to me asked whether we should go outside and mend the aerial. A few months before I would probably have said 'yes', but after the experiences of the past months my rather cowardly reply was' No. We will wait until all is quiet'. Later on there was one of those magical musical moments. It was dark and the front line was quiet, when through the air came the sound of a lone piper playing in the Black Watch reserve position. It was not a battle tune but a gentle melody reminiscent of the lone piper standing on the castle at the Edinburgh Tattoo; a most bewitching moment. 'Isn't that great?' I asked Gunner Page. 'Yes,' he replied. 'It's two miles away.'

At this time, the Chinese were launching their 'Peace Offensive' and during the night would get up to our wire and attach colourful pamphlets tempting the soldiers to defect. The pamphlets had the title 'Fight against Imperialism': 'You are told you are in Korea to fight aggression, but who is the Aggressor – American Billionaires.' There were also copies of *Peace News* which included articles entitled 'Quakers Appeal for Peace in Korea', 'US Airmen Refuse to Fly', and an extract from a letter from a mother in Cheshire to her local newspaper headed: 'My Heart goes out to those Lonely Lads. Bring an End to this Terrible War and Bring Peace to this England of ours.' There were also Safe Conduct Passes issued by the Headquarters of the Chinese People's Volunteers. They contained pictures of happy, smiling United Nations Prisoners of War and in Chinese with an English translation said:

> The Bearer, regardless of nationality or rank is to be treated in accordance with our policy of leniency to prisoners of war and escorted to the nearest headquarters of the Korean People's Army or the Chinese People's Volunteers. He is to be guaranteed –
>
> Security of Life
> Retention of all personal belongings
> Freedom from maltreatment or abuse
> Medical care if wounded or ill
>
> Signed

KIM IL SUNG
SUPREME COMMANDER KOREA PEOPLE'S ARMY
PENG THE-HUAI
COMMANDER PEOPLE'S CHINESE VOLUNTEERS

It was interesting how many officers and soldiers had retained one of these leaflets in their wallets after the war had ended. Not, they would quickly protest, that they ever considered surrendering, but maybe under certain circumstances it would not do any harm to have this document on their person. I was one such officer and still have the pass. Well you never know!

One annoying part of this peace attack was that in the early hours of the morning, whilst it was dark and quiet, came the siren sound of a young girl singing love songs followed by calls to join her. The troops called her 'Pyongyang Sally' and she sounded very close so once I tried a few rounds' gunfire to disrupt her harmony but, as the laconic Gunner Page remarked: 'You'll have to be damned lucky to hit a microphone.' Other broadcasts as recorded in the Duke of Wellington's Regimental War Diary were: 'Why do you bomb our villages day after day? Why don't you go home? America started this war; you British have no reason to fight here, but we are fighting for our lives. For the sake of your mothers and children, leave Korea. Give yourself up because within five days there will be an attack.'

Whilst in the OP we could observe the contribution of the Sound Ranging Troop of 15 Locating and Light Ack Ack Battery. This Battery had three sound ranging sections, A, B, and C, each able to lay our four microphones equipped with recorders using teledeltos paper. By 1953, given the static line of defence, the three troops had sound-ranging capability across the whole of the Divisional Front and a large log of recorded targets. When there was distinguishable sound of an individual Chinese gun as opposed to a rumble of gunfire, the section officer would switch on the microphones and was able to get a triangulation of the firing guns location. He could then judge whether the shooting came from a mortar that was on a reverse slope and therefore could not be hit, or it was a gun firing directly at our lines. If an accurate location was obtained, the section commander would give a fire order directly to 74 (Battle Axe Company), which was the designated Counter Bombardment Battery for a single gun target. When the gun fired, the recorder was switched on at the appropriate time in order to record the sound wave of the shell landing. The gun would then be ranged visually to destroy the enemy weapon. When this was achieved, the order would be given, 'Record as target'. The battery would then work out the location, range and bearing to the target, give it a target number and pass the details to the divisional counter bombardment officer (DCBO) at HQRA. This recording of counter bombardment targets was extremely useful and was used extensively both during the Battles of The Hook and when patrols ran into trouble. The microphones were mounted on a base, which looked rather like a Christmas cake with wires attached. Not surprisingly, therefore, they could be mistaken for mines, and there were instances of them being hooked to an armoured vehicle and towed away, and of infantrymen crawling gingerly, but bravely forward to cut the wires, much to the annoyance of the Sound Section Linesman who had to go out and repair the damage.

One evening the company commander briefed that there may be a 'runner' passing through the company position that night. The message did not, however, get to a Kingsman in the forward platoon who had a serious fright when a darkly clad figure ran silently past him through a hole in the wire and disappeared towards the Chinese Lines. These 'runners' were Koreans who volunteered to return to the Chinese lines and gather information. A Joint United States and British Special Forces unit based on the island of Cho-Do controlled them, and Major Ellery Anderson, an SAS Officer, who twice parachuted clandestinely into North Korea, was in charge. Serving in this Detachment was Staff Sergeant Clifford Jackson, Intelligence Corps. Sergeant Jackson had served in the Royal Fusiliers in Italy during the war and had been awarded the DCM. He then transferred to the Intelligence Corps and from October 1951 until May 1953, was a member of this unit known as the 1st Commonwealth Division Special Detachment. The detachment was responsible for selecting, training and then sending Koreans back into North Korea to carry out sabotage and information gathering. Sergeant Jackson went into North Korea himself, and for this was awarded the Military Medal and the American Silver Star. Sergeant John Wells Intelligence Corps was another member of this unit who was awarded the American Bronze Star for 'Recruiting, training and infiltrating Koreans back into North Korea.' The men selected were all from North Korea and were trained in weapon handling just south of the Imjin by 904 Field Security Section in a secure area marked 'DANGER – OUTBREAK OF SMALLPOX'. We called them 'line crossers' or 'guerrillas', but when caught by the North Koreans they were shot as 'spies'. Given the political situation still existing in North Korea, their activities behind the lines are still graded 'Top Secret'.

Every night B Company sent out patrols. Mervyn would brief the route and confirm the weapons to be carried. For food they would have tins of self-warming soups, and for warmth many had bought their own battery-operated small metal 'warmers' to distribute around their bodies. It was never completely dark at night as the American Field Artillery searchlight batteries were always in action. Their searchlights had 60-inch lights with 8 million candlepower, could throw a beam 20,000 yards, and gave a soft reflected light from the clouds. Mervyn Ryder was ambiguous about the value of this reflected light; it could aid navigation but did increase his patrols' vulnerability. The only other light came from a single pencil-like searchlight beam from the site of the Panmunjom Armistice Talks which was continually switched on, we were told, to ensure the site was not inadvertently bombed by either side. My role each night was to agree a Fire Plan to give covering fire if a patrol ran into trouble. As the patrol might be lying in close proximity to a Chinese patrol, Mervyn agreed a communication procedure with his Kingsmen; when he wanted to be in contact, he would very, very quietly whisper his question and without speaking the patrol radioman would press his transmitting switch once for a 'yes' reply, and twice for a 'no' reply. If they did bump into the Chinese and suffered casualties, the code word 'Cups' would be given for men killed and 'Plates' for any wounded. These code words were used far too often and seemed more poignant given that the talks at Panmunjom seemed to be reaching agreement. Brought up on stories of infantry soldiers at El Alamein and Normandy 'crossing the start line and moving into the smoke', there was a supposition that, dangerous as it was, the advancing soldiers must have felt the comfort of the nearness and comradeship of a large group. This was not the case in Korea; the patrols of four National Servicemen, often commanded by a Corporal or Lance Corporal, had to go out through one of very few gaps in the wire, lie up in the paddy in spots where many had hidden before, were certainly known to the Chinese, and could never be certain if an ambush was waiting for them. It was a cold, lonely and frightening task. Watching the patrols of young men being briefed always left me with the feeling again of pride, respect and admiration.

On 24 July we were told that the Armistice talks at Panmunjom had been concluded and that on the 27th the Armistice would be signed, but this was still not certain. On 24 July when looking out of the OP, I saw two Chinese soldiers in the valley evidently laying line. There had been little activity that morning, so I decided to return the compliment we had received from the Chinese gunner and give three rounds to disturb their line laying. I ordered Baker Troop into action to prepare for three rounds' gun fire. Somewhat to my surprise, the battery command post officer authorised a battery target and so it would be eight guns. In order to avoid any accidents I added 100 yards to the range then, to my amazement, the adjutant came on the air and authorised a regimental target i.e. twenty-four guns. I added another 200 yards to the range. At this moment, Major Beard, who was commanding the company, came running into the OP. He had heard the authorisation for a regimental shoot in front of his position and wondered what on earth was happening. I did not know. Then more amazement as a divisional shoot was authorised; seventy-two guns. So I added another 200 yards to the range, then a corps shoot was authorised and I added yet more range; then authorisation for all guns in neighbouring corps to fire. I added more range and over a hundred and twenty guns then fired at an unknown target at least a mile behind the two Chinese linesman. The whole distant skyline became a mass of smoke.

Later I heard the reason for this episode. Although the Armistice talks had been concluded, it was still not certain that the Chinese would actually sign the Agreement. UN Headquarters had decided, therefore, to demonstrate to the Chinese that although they were ready to conclude the agreement, if the Chinese did not do so the UN was quite ready to continue the fight. My claim, therefore, is to have fired more guns in one shoot, called a 'Victor target', than any British Officer since the crossing of the Rhine.

On the day the Armistice was due to be signed there was an air of uneasy calm; neither the Chinese nor us did any firing. Darkness fell, and we waited for 2200 hrs when we were told the ceasefire would take effect. At 2159 hrs, the Chinese hills opposite looked just as dark, remote, mysterious and sinister as ever. Suddenly, on the hour, we heard the familiar plopping sound of Chinese mortars and waited for the explosions to follow. But they did not come. The sky was filled with colour; the mortar bombs were smoke bombs not explosive bombs. A ragged cheer went up from the British lines and, totally against all the rules, the sky was filled with every sort of coloured smoke, as in return our soldiers fired their smoke bombs, lit flares and fired Verey lights. There was a glorious moment of brilliance, then a deep, deep silence. I left the OP, and for the first time stood on top and through the darkness came the sound of a song. It rippled along our front line from platoon to platoon. It was spontaneous; it was emotional; it was, 'There'll always be an England'.

Next day Mervyn and I again sat on the roof of the OP looking over the valley. The Chinese side was quiet, but there were reports that some soldiers had crossed over and met the Chinese and exchanged gifts. We decided to go down ourselves without our revolvers, and look at the ground that had been so unapproachable for so long. Mervyn found the boot of one of the soldiers who had been badly wounded the week before, and then up popped two Chinese soldiers. All four froze and all eyes went to see if anyone was armed; no one was. Smiles and photographs followed, then we returned and I have always wondered if they were the two soldiers I had tried to kill two days before, and whose presence had resulted in a Victor target.

That day, Easy Three Gun in 107 Battery was told they were to fire the last round of the War, and it they did with great ceremony. It was perhaps not so certain that this was the case, however, for when we were back in Hong Kong, there were at least four other cartridge cases engraved 'THE LAST ROUND'.

CHAPTER NINE

Baker Troop Occupies the Kansas Line

A few days later we evacuated the OP and drove back to build fresh gun pits. The King's Regiment marched back. A new man now became the most important man in the troop, not Gunner Prince who was the ace on the artillery board, not Gunner Corbett who was the Ace No. 3 on the guns, not Bombardier Riley who could get any engine started in any weather; it was Gunner Bland who could paint signs. In our new positions everything had to have an emblazed sign, 'Command Post', 'Troop Store', each gun position and even the Thunder Boxes all required the complicated Minden Rose and uniform red and blue lettering. One day Gunner Bland was absent from parade and a rather evasive Sergeant Major Wroot admitted that during a convivial meeting with Mr Wells the Battery Sergeant Major in the mess, he had agreed that Gunner Bland could be attached to Battery Head Quarters for a week. It was essential, Sergeant Major Wroot said, that our battery signs should be the best in the regiment and I am sure our troop gained some advantage in return.

The Panmunjom Agreement had stipulated that both sides should move back four kilometres from their existing positions, and that a demilitarised zone should be established in which no fortifications could be erected. The work of the troop now revolved around destroying all the existing constructions and moving back to a new line called The Kansas Line. When knocking down Baker Troop command post there was an incident that for sixty years has left me with an icy feeling of fear. As the petrol stove was dismantled we pulled away the ammunition box on which it had been rested and, as it seemed heavy, clicked open the catches – it was full of red and white super-charge explosive bags. These were the bags that were added to the cartridge case if extra distance to a target was required. Given the frequency that these stoves burst into flames, no imagination was required to guess what the effect of an explosion would have been in the confined space of our small command post dugout. The stove was in place when we arrived. Who can guess if it was a gross act of carelessness or a North Korean sympathiser working for the British Army?

Suddenly there was a realisation what a beautiful country Korea was; a land where, for hundreds of years, there had been culture and cultivation. Focussed up to now on gun pits and dugouts, it was a delightful revelation to look around and see why Korea is called the 'Land of the Morning Calm'. The weather was good, the air fresh and clean, and the gunners enjoyed digging gun pits along the new Kansas Line. It was a remote area full of flaming maples, purple azaleas, and multi-coloured wild flowers, and we were left undisturbed. There was a lot of birdsong though it seemed to me that the most numerous birds were magpies and pheasants. The gunners knew that when they finished the pits they would be deployed on other tasks, so the pace of digging was gentle. We built a new OP overlooking a new valley and for the first time I was amazed to see a continuous flight of helicopters carrying heavy concrete lintels and huge logs slung underneath in net and webbing bags. A very difficult task was made very easy. The tempo of work slackened significantly. Captain Derek Richardson, the REME officer at Brigade, noticed that during the war when he went to bed the fitters would be hard at work and when he awoke the repairs would still be going on. Skiving – i.e. trying to get out of working – was a peacetime habit. Soldiers had been trained to do a job and were self-motivated to complete a task without supervision. When the ceasefire came into effect, the motivation disappeared.

Baker Troop continued to support the King's Regiment and I was appointed the FOO to Major Tom Twaddle, known as 'Tam'. Our role was as a Counter-Attack Force which meant panting up very steep hills and driving off a mythical enemy. Tam was quite elderly at the time, but was always first to the top. He had fought in Italy and

Burma during the Second World War, and after Korea he became commanding officer of the Hong Kong Regiment. On his retirement he was 'mine host' of the Cameronian hotel in Lanarkshire and always made a special point of welcoming ex-Kingsmen.

Every unit had a number of Korean soldiers/labourers attached to them. The soldiers in the Infantry Battalions were totally integrated into the platoons, shared the same trenches, the same dangers and took their full part in patrolling and manning the gun pits. Their bravery steadily earned the respect and affection of the British soldiers. Most could not speak English and 99 per cent were called 'Kim', so in the Black Watch they were given Roman names – Nero, Pompeii, Caesar, etc. They also wore the famous 'Red Hackle' which was the unique right of the Black Watch as the Senior Highland Regiment. The story goes that when a reinforcement to the Black Watch arrived at Pusan and saw a Korean soldier wearing the Red Hackle, he was heard to say: 'Hey Jock – You must have been here a hell'va long time!' We had a few young Koreans attached to the Troop who managed to get uniforms cut down to their size and were extremely useful in helping around the gun lines. To solve the problem of identification, Sergeant Major Wroot had the bright idea of painting a number on the helmet of the Koreans, although after some aggravation he did not include number one or number ten.

We did see groups of refugees moving around the country and there was positive information that the North Koreans had infiltrated their agents to mingle clandestinely with these groups. Members of 904 Intelligence Section had developed a good technique to discover these agents. They would stop a refugee column and then, through their interpreters, ask all grandmothers and grandfathers to move aside; then all the women and children. Finally, they would ask the grandmothers to pick out their relatives and this would leave a number of single males who could be investigated in detail. This selection process provided a good filter, but given that so few United Nations soldiers spoke Korean, the interviewing or interrogation had to be done using an interpreter which slowed down the process and reduced the impact. North Korean agents shot dead Sergeant Edward Hall, Intelligence Corps, who was meeting a contact in Seoul, and Sergeant R. Davies received a Commander in Chief's Commendation for catching a North Korean who had blown up a British ammunition dump.

During the war we had very little contact with the Korean people as there was a 'stay behind line' which the Koreans were theoretically not allowed to cross. This was known to the troops as the 'No Skirts Line', although we did see elderly men in high hats and white flowing dresses with wooden 'A' shaped frames on their backs carrying huge bundles of hay. The women seemed dignified and wore traditional dress. I cannot remember seeing a girl in a skirt, but was assured there were plenty in Seoul. After the war it became clear that, in spite of being insulated from the outside world for so long by the authoritarian control of the Japanese, within this ancient and cultured people there was already emerging a younger generation ready, capable and determined to move their country into the economic freedom of the modern world. In December 1952 Seoul was a picture of devastation, but by the autumn of 1953 there was already an air of industry, energy and reconstruction and, as is usual in the Far East, the schoolchildren were immaculately turned out. On the way back from a visit to Seoul there was a NAAFI Road House where it was possible to buy hot drinks and snacks, and a small gift shop with a selection of Japanese dolls etc. that the shop would send home on your behalf. They also ran a type of 'Inter Flora' service. NAAFI mobile canteens also visited the gun positions and were always welcomed, especially as they sold Mars Bars and Crunchy bars. They were always well-stocked, as sales from the Mobile Canteens did not have to pay the 10 per cent dividend to unit funds that were required from sales in their shops. Throughout our tour we had an excellent postal service. Shaun Jackson's mother complained to the Post Office in Folkestone, Kent, that a parcel she had sent had not arrived. Very shortly afterwards a soldier from the Royal Engineer 206 Post Unit arrived at the gun position to check if the parcel had arrived. Shaun was most impressed.

While in the Kansas Line one of our officers was detached to go to Panmunjom to supervise the repatriation of prisoners of war, and on several occasions he asked me to go with him. It was a moving experience; we did not know what time each day the Chinese would begin the exchange, or how many would be allowed to cross over 'The

Bridge of No Return' or whom they would be. The door would open and in would come the ex-prisoners clutching small bags of possessions. They were not certain that it was really true that they were free; so many times in the past the Chinese had given them the impression that they were to be released and then it had not happened. Tense, concerned looks, broke into huge smiles; laughter erupted and all was joy. Regimental Sergeant Major Hobbs of the Gloucestershires came through looking rather gaunt, but with an air of quiet assurance that he was still the RSM and was quite ready to take his place in front of a battalion parade. The ex-prisoners went through a medical inspection, had a haircut, a luxurious hot bath, were given a completely new set of clothing, and were then offered a meal of their choice. The Americans universally asked for a steak; the British favourite was sausage and chips or fish and chips. Before sailing home the ex-prisoners went to Japan and were interviewed in the British Repatriated POW Integrated (Intelligence) Unit.

On the Communist side there was also a welcoming party with flags, banners and pretty girls offering flowers to greet the North Korean and Chinese ex-prisoners as they walked towards their countrymen. Many of these took off all the clothes they had been given, including their boots and threw them away. It was their last act of defiance. At the time I thought how stupid, the poor guys will regret doing that. Subsequently, however, I felt they were being both shrewd and prudent – the Russians sent to the Gulags, all those who had been prisoners of war, even those who had been critically wounded when they were captured. The ex-Chinese prisoners knew that having been in US hands they would be ideologically suspect and it would be best to publicly and quickly demonstrate they had not been subverted and remained positively anti-US Imperialists.

At Panmunjom there was a group of American nurses and our officer asked if they could be invited back to our Mess for a meal. Johnny King-Martin called a battery mess meeting and put it to the vote. As Wines Member I asked what drinks should be prepared and with great confidence our Panmunjom Representative explained that the nurses would drink very little and advised the preparation of a large quantity of a non-alcoholic punch. The vote was carried, and great efforts were made to improve the decor of the mess tent for this unprecedented visit by ladies. The big evening arrived; the door opened and in advanced a large bosomy blonde. Johnny moved across and in his most polished manner introduced himself: 'I am the Battery Commander, Major Johnny King-Martin. May I offer you a drink?' 'Sure Johnny' was the reply. 'I'll have a large scotch.' It was a great party and everyone enjoyed the evening apart from our Battery Commander who saw the whole of the Mess' month's whisky ration rapidly disappear so rapidly that I had to send to the Sergeants' Mess for a resupply, an arrangement which cost us a great deal in the following months. A more successful party was the celebration of Minden Day. The battery was lined up and the battery commander walked along the line presenting each soldier with a rose to be placed in their hat. This was followed by a grand meal which, following the tradition of Christmas Day, was served by the officers, warrant officers and senior NCOs.

There was an unpleasant surprise one day when a staff officer arrived to check our stores, known as the G1098 stores. As we had taken over from 14 Field Regiment without any formal handover and any losses had been replaced without fuss, the reality between what Baker Troop had, and what we should officially have, differed hugely. Thankfully, the staff officer was sympathetic to our discrepancies and gave time for the accounting system to be rectified. The three items which caused most heartache were compasses, watches and binoculars. He would accept the loss of gun and vehicle stores from enemy shelling but these three items had to be found.

Two mandatory inspections were reinitiated; foot inspections and crotch inspections. Foot inspections were fairly simple; the gunners would lie on their beds, take off their boots and show their feet. Sergeant Major Wroot, the Detachment Commander, and I would then look at the feet. The aim was to detect athlete's foot which was common, but which could be stopped quickly by the use of foot powder. If the feet looked grubby, Sergeant Major Wroot would use colourful language to point this out, not to the gunner, but to the Detachment Commander. We only did a crotch inspection once. The gunners had to stand up and expose their private parts which provoked a lot of amusement and ribald comments. The aim was not to detect disease, but to check for the red rash of tinea. I am not sure what happened in the other troops, but it seemed an invasion of privacy and somehow not appropriate in Baker Troop, and so, with the tacit agreement of Sergeant Major Wroot, we quietly dropped crotch inspections.

Life began to adopt a peacetime flavour. We did not have a regimental mess; each battery was self-contained. We had our own Quonset Mess Hut, similar to a Nissan Hut, and we lived within this 'family bubble'. There were visits to other units, inter-battery sports, a renewal of bonds with other members of the Regiment, but no apprehension that the war might start again and we never talked of our experiences in the war. It took over fifty years before friends in the Regiment felt comfortable to discuss the stress and tension of past battles. Each battery adopted its own evening recreation; in 12 (Minden) Battery we played poker and although the stakes were extremely low and it was only possible to lose £5 in a month, it was taken very seriously and there was an extreme sense of competition. In 45 Battery they played Bridge and considered themselves very superior, and in 107 Battery they played 'Vingt et Un' and were considered rather plebeian. When we joined the other batteries for a party it inevitably ended with the full-throated singing of rugby songs; the favourite referring to the exploits of two-dozen ladies from Inverness. HQRA ran a famous roulette evening which attracted officers from all nationalities. The drinks were free, but the chips were charged at a 10 per cent discount. It was very profitable for HQRA.

The soldiers soon learned the local language, or at least knew No 1 was 'good', No 10 was 'bad', Toxon, 'a lot'; Scochie, 'a little'; Chop Chop, 'hurry up', and if asked the question, 'You want Jig a Jig?' knew that it meant a short happy time and a long uncomfortable time. Major parties were held, and one in particular became famous. It was the farewell parade of 1 Royal Tank Regiment. After a powerfully impressive drive-past of Centurion tanks, plus the command vehicles, we went to the Mess where the only drink on offer was Black Velvet, a mixture of Guinness and Champagne. This, we were told, was a regimental custom in the Royal Tank Regiment and was based on the colour of their berets. I have the memory of an officer climbing astride the barrel of a tank like a jockey, then slowly sliding upside down, falling directly on his head and laying deathly still. There was a worried silence until a friend rushed up with a resuscitating glass of Black Velvet.

One of the advantages of being able to travel was the opportunity to buy from local shops. It was very difficult to get Won, the Korean currency, but there was a great demand for empty beer bottles. Shaun Jackson was detailed, therefore, to collect all the 'empties' and exchange them for items required for his Officers' Mess, such as tables and comfortable chairs. This was a forbidden practice which the NAAFI tried hard to stop and gained the cooperation of the Military Police. As the price for the bottles increased, the closer the bottles got to Seoul, a 'risk assessment' had to be made; less risk equalled less money and less risk of detection; more risk equalled more money and more risk of detection. Once, when Shaun was returning from such a trip, his jeep turned over and was completely destroyed. It could have been a very expensive affair, but acting on advice he took two bottles of whisky to the nearest American vehicle park and returned with a brand new jeep. His Battery Commander assumed a 'Nelson's Eye'. Baker Troop also had reason to be grateful that our Battery Commander had a 'Nelson's Eye' as we were unique in the Regiment for receiving a Commander in Chief United Nations Forces Japan Official Reprimand, having been found guilty of 'drifting'. One day, when leading the Troop, we had encountered great difficulty in maintaining radio communications. I had therefore ordered 'Follow Me', and voicing a tuning and netting call, gradually changed the frequency upwards until we got perfect reception. Three months later a dispatch rider appeared with a large envelope containing this Official Reprimand from Tokyo. It was countersigned by the United States General Commanding the Eight Army in Korea, the General commanding the British Commonwealth Division the Commander 29 Brigade, and was endorsed by my own Commanding Officer. My Battery Commander, Major Johnnie King-Martin read it and tore it up.

The gunners gradually left the troop as their demobilization date came round. The departure of one NCO caused me great concern and the incident had an effect on the rest of my service. Sergeant B. was the only No.1 who had not served during the war. He was young, forceful, and articulate and had a natural power of command. In army terms he was 'outstanding'. He said he wanted to leave Korea to be with his wife and new baby. We met several times officially and then alone with bottles of Asahi beer. I knew that one day he was sure to be an RSM and it seemed incomprehensible that he would give up the chance of such a fine career, but he was adamant and left. As he drove away I was devastated, but I learned a lesson. The result was that for the next thirty-five years when constantly being told that the resignation of an officer or NCO would have a catastrophic effect on the army, it made no impact. The army is like a pond, into which a stone has been thrown; after a resignation a ripple occurs, but then someone else picks up the job and the departure is soon forgotten.

It was time to look in retrospect at how well the regiment had done in the war. It was very satisfying that in the official histories of the Thai, French, Turk and American Battalions, all were fulsome in their praise of the artillery fire support they had received. More important, perhaps, was that the three battalions of 29 Brigade – the Black Watch, the Duke of Wellington's Regiment and the King's Regiment – consistently and fulsomely acknowledged the effect on their battles of the fire from the regiment. The pattern of these battles was always the same. It would open with a Chinese bombardment consisting of heavy concentrations of artillery and mortar fire to blow holes in the minefield and barbed wire. At H Hour the Chinese would emerge from caves or concealed trenches as close to our front line as possible, and launch a terrifying attack with screaming, shouting infantry to the accompaniment of whistles and bugles. In spite of coordinated tank, machine gun and mortar fire, they consistently broke through the defences and were often soon occupying the forward positions. Their artillery fire then moved to our rear areas to destroy reinforcement routes and disrupt counter-attacks.

The role of our artillery was initially to provide counter bombardment shoots then, with as much fire power as possible, generally using airburst shells, destroy the advancing Chinese in the time between they left their dugouts and reached our positions. Pre-arranged targets were then called to destroy those Chinese who had managed to get on top of our positions hoping that our infantry knew what was going to happen and allowing them time to conceal themselves in deep, well-protected dugouts. The artillery fire would then use smoke and high explosive to support our counter-attacks, finally moving to their rear areas to disrupt their counter-attacks.

This artillery support was provided in spite of the complexity of having four different countries forming the Divisional and Attached Artillery. Every country – Canada, New Zealand, the USA and Britain – had different terms of service and different legal codes, and each retained complete power over such things as postings and discipline. Each country had a commander of its own, but by July 1953 the Baker Troop OP officer could call for fire from every gun and mortar in the division, including the 8-inch howitzers of the US 17 Battery and the 'Persuaders' of the US 936 Battery, and rounds would be on the ground within two minutes. It was a remarkable example of gunner communication and cooperation and it was successfully done time and time again. A poignant demonstration of the infantry appreciation of this support came when, on leaving Korea, the Duke of Wellington's Regiment held its final parade at the Pusan Military Cemetery, and as well as reading out the names of those in the Battalion who had died, also included the names of the gunners from 20th Field Regiment RA.

The 20th Field Regiment RA gained no great publicity; there was no glorious page in the Royal Regimental History to match the epic battles of Corunna, Colenso, Nery, El Alemein and Imjin, and this may be because when gaining historical immorality, two factors come into play – the number of casualties and the number of decorations. The casualty list of 20th Field Regiment in comparison with the infantry battalions was very small, although to us just as sad. The list of decorations is, however, significant. During the war only two immediate gallantry awards were awarded; the MC given to Captain Gordon for his contribution in the OP during the Battle of The Hook, and the MM to Sergeant Onyett for his gallantry and determination on the death of Captain Bill Miller. Post-war the decorations went to the Commanding Officer Colonel Geoffrey Brennan who was awarded the DSO, and the three Battery Commanders, each of whom received the MC. The fact that all our senior officers were honoured in this way was public acknowledgment that the regiment had done its job and had maintained the high professional traditions of the Royal Regiment in battle. Two other soldiers from the regiment were awarded Military Medals; Bombardier Geoffrey Machen and Gunner William Elcoat. Both were Linesmen in 45 Battery and had shown exceptional bravery during the battle of The Hook by repairing the telephone lines which were continually being cut by the heavy Chinese shelling. Six members of the regiment were mentioned in dispatches. Thirty-eight years later, an historian researching the period when 107 Battery supported the French Battalion, discovered that Colonel Brennan, Major Scott Shore and his two Troop Commanders, Captains Hugh Fairgrieve and John Morgan, had been awarded the Croix de Guerre, but that the British Authorities had failed to pass on this information. In a delightful gesture, the French Ambassador gave 'a splendid party' in the French Embassy in London and made the delayed presentation.

It is very important to say that the artillery support we provided could only have been achieved with the help of the Logistic Corps. The RAOC made sure we never ran short of food or ammunition; the RASC never faltered in making sure this food and ammunition arrived on time; the REME were always with us making sure we could move and fire. As a personal conclusion, my highest accolade would go to the RAOC. This was a war of supply, and in spite of enormous difficulties we were never short of supplies.

Gradually the time came when we were to leave Korea and return to Hong Kong. The moment I had waited for eventually arrived and up the path leading to Baker Troop Command Post came the relieving officer from 42 Field Regiment. I took him round the area and then said: 'Well it's all yours now. Here's a bottle of whisky as a present. Happy Christmas. Good luck and good-bye.' The Korean experience had come to an end.

Part Two

Reaction to the War

* * *

CHAPTER TEN

Who Won the War?

It is traditional at the end of a war to ask the question 'Who won?' The Russians felt they had won. They had provided large quantities of weapons and ammunition, much of it of Second World War vintage; they had lost a few pilots but no soldiers, and North Korea remained as before under their control. They had watched the USA spend vast amounts of money and suffer thousands of casualties but with no territorial gain. Given the great success of the North Korean forces in June 1950 and the Chinese success in October 1950, they also felt it would encourage other communist armies, like that in Vietnam, in the belief that the mighty USA could be defeated.

The Chinese Communist Government felt it had won. They had believed that MacArthur was going to launch an attack into China combined with an assault from Taiwan, and that if this attack had run into serious difficulties MacArthur might well have resorted to the atom bomb and this had not happened. They had proved to their own people that they could defeat the combined forces of the United Nations; that they had removed forever the threat from Chiang Kai Shek, and that they were now the indisputable leaders of China and were recognised in the United Nations as a sovereign state.

The Americans felt they had won. It had been a military success. First there was the remarkable feat of moving a peacetime army from Japan to Korea at very short notice and successfully halting the North Korean invasion, then the brilliance and audacity of the landing at Inchon which had led to the defeat of the North Korean Army, then the defeat of a huge, invading Chinese Army and forcing them back to the 38th Parallel. It had also been a major political success. The fear in Washington as expounded by Mr Dulles, had been the 'domino factor', i.e. if any county in the Far East was allowed to fall under Communist domination this would have a knock-on effect on neighbouring countries. This had been prevented. What General Charles Willoughby, the Senior Intelligence Officer on General Macarthur's staff, called the 'threat of Mongoloid-Pan-Slavism under the guise of communism' had been stopped. By the end of the war Japan had become a sovereign state and had raised an army which could counter any armed aggression from the USSR. The Nationalist Government in Taiwan was now established, and by putting the 7th Fleet in the Straits of Formosa there was no likelihood of an invasion by either side and thus the risk of war with China had been reduced. South Korea had been rescued and threat of invasion from the North no longer existed. And finally, as General Willoughby said: 'Of even greater significance is the revelation that this new enemy, Red China, of such exaggerated and vaunted military power, lacks the industrial capacity essential to modern war.' From the American perspective all good news.

The British felt they had won. Before the Second World War British interest in the Korean Peninsular was minimal. Britain had maintained a pro-consul in Wosan and there were some missionaries in the north of the country, but apart from some trade in gold there was little contact. Following the division of the Korean Peninsular in 1945 and the emergence of the two separate Korean States, Britain, in common with most Western countries, had recognised the Republic of Korea (ROK) as the 'only legitimate government on the Peninsular', although this recognition did not endorse the ROK claim to the whole Peninsular. There was, therefore, no vital reason that necessitated Britain to go to war in Korea. Prime Minister Attlee, however, supported Washington's view that the spread of communism by force was unacceptable, especially given British interests in Hong Kong, Malaya and Singapore. There was the painful memory that in the recent past, failure to stop aggression had twice before led to greater conflict, i.e. when Mussolini had invaded Ethiopia and when Hitler had invaded Czechoslovakia. Military support to save South Korea was therefore seen to be a sensible good thing to do, especially under the banner of a new and revitalised United Nations. When the Cabinet Secretary at the end of a cabinet meeting remarked: 'Korea is rather a distant obligation, Prime Minister,' Mr Atlee had replied: 'Distant yes, but none the less an obligation.' This explained the British decision to go to war in Korea but it did not explicitly commit Britain to cross the 38th Parallel and destroy the Government in the north. However, when General MacArthur *did* cross the Parallel, Britain made no objection, and on 25 September 1950 the British Foreign Secretary Mr Ernest Bevin, in an address to the United Nations said: 'There must no longer be South Koreans and North Koreans, but just Koreans who must be encouraged to work together to rebuild their country with the advice and support of the United Nations.' Although his aim had not been achieved by July 1953, Britain saw it as a victory that the North Koreans had been pushed back to their original positions and that South Korea remained free. Most importantly, this had been achieved without an escalation into a Third World War as, theoretically, the Korean War had not involved Russia or China. The British Army had fought well and won some glorious battles.

Australia had certainly won. The Australian Army had gained more Battle Honours for their service in Korea including Pakchon and Kapyong, which had added to many other past honours including the Anzac Landing at Gallipoli, Tobruk and the Kokoda Trail. All three Battalions of the Royal Australian Regiment had taken part and it was a matter of justifiable pride that the Australian Army was feared by the Chinese Army and respected by every other Contingent in the United Nations Force. They had lost 411 men, 1,216 were wounded, 21 were taken Prisoners of War, and 2 RAR had been awarded the US Presidential Citation for their gallantry at Kapyong; 77 Squadron RAAF had fought continually throughout the war, mainly in the dangerous role of ground attack, and had lost forty-one men with six being taken as prisoners of war. They qualified for the Battle Honour 'Korea 1950-1953', and among an impressive number of awards were three DSOs and fifty-three DFCs.

The Canadians had certainly won. All four regiments of the Canadian Army that took part in the war earned the Battle Honour 'Korea 1951-53', and in special recognition of their exceptional gallantry in 1951, the 2nd Battalion Princess Patricia's Canadian Light Infantry was also awarded the Battle Honour Kapyong, plus a US Presidential Citation. The Canadian regiments in Korea had maintained the fine traditions for gallantry of professional capability that had been recognised by the past Battle Honours of Beaumont Hamel, Vimy Ridge, Juno Beach, the Falaise Gap and many more. They had lost 344, 1,212 were wounded and 12 taken as Prisoners of War. The same went for the Canadian logistic units, and in the *History of the Royal Artillery* it states: 'The superb drivers and mates of the Canadian Transport Company of the Royal Canadian Army Service Corps never failed to negotiate by night and day the most treacherous and icy of roads to reach the guns, help unload and then go back for more.'

New Zealand had certainly won; 16 Field Regiment RNZA, as a volunteer unit had fought from the very beginning of the War to the very end. They served in 27 Infantry Brigade and 29 Commonwealth Brigade, and for their courageous artillery fire support to the 6th ROK Division at Kapyong, were awarded the Republic of Korea Presidential Citation. They had made a remarkable professional contribution which followed the traditions of Gallipoli, The Somme, El Alamein and Casino, amongst others. They had thirty-four killed, seventy-nine wounded and one Prisoner of War.

South Africa had certainly won. Its main contribution to the United Nations was 2 Squadron South African Air Force that had proved to be an outstanding fighter squadron. The squadron served in Korea from November 1950 until December 1953, and were attached to the 18th USAF Fighter Bomber Group. Initially, they flew P-51 Mustangs but were later re-equipped with F-86 Sabre aircraft and flew a total 12,405 sorties. The 18th Group earned a Distinguished Unit Citation for flying 6,500 combat sorties, while operating from damaged runways to counter the enemy's 1951

Spring Offensive. The South African pilots became renowned for their courage in low-level ground attack missions which became more and more dangerous as the Chinese improved their anti-aircraft capability. As a sad testimony to the bravery and determination of 2 Squadron, out of a total of 829 members who served in Korea, 35 pilots were killed, 16 were wounded and 8 were shot down and taken prisoner. Also lost were seventy-four of their ninety-four Mustangs and four of their twenty Sabres. Not surprisingly, the 'Flying Cheetahs' were awarded the Republic of Korea Presidential Citation, the United States Presidential Unit Citation, and many other awards and decorations including three Legions of Merit and fifty Distinguished Flying Crosses. One very special and moving tribute came from the Commanding Officer of the USAF 18th Fighter Bomber Wing who issued the following directive:

> In memory of our gallant South African comrades, it is hereby established as a new policy, that at all Retreat Ceremonies held by this Wing the playing of our National Anthem should be preceded by playing the introductory bars of the South African National Anthem, 'Die Stem van Suid-Afrika.' All personnel of this Wing will render the same honours to this Anthem as our own.

What a nice gesture. I was present at Pyonyang when several of the South African pilots were released. Bearded and boisterous is a good description.

India had certainly won. It had decided to support the United Nations and did so immediately and in a most practical way. The 60th Parachute Field Ambulance served in Korea for three-and-a-half years, a longer period of service in Korea than any other unit. As well as providing medical support for all the overseas United Nations Contingents they helped the ROK Army and the local civilians, and well deserved the title 'The Maroon Angels'. Twelve members who jumped with the American Airborne Forces were awarded US parachute wings, and the Field Ambulance received unit citations from the ROK Army, the US Army and the Commonwealth Division. On their return to India they were awarded the President's Trophy by the first President of the Republic of India, Dr Rajendra Prasad, an honour that has not been given to any other unit since that time.

All the Commonwealth Contingents had done their job. When they returned home their governments and people could say: 'We asked you to risk your lives in order to stop aggression and you succeeded. Thank you.'

The South Koreans felt to some degree they had won. The arbitrary line drawn on the map which had no geographical or ethnic basis, and which, although it had been imposed upon them divided communities and families in a totally illogical manner, had been preserved. Military occupation by their fellow Koreans who lived in the north and had a different political agenda had been prevented. The natural pride of the people of Korea and determination to be independent after so many decades could now, for the first time, be allowed to develop in the South. Rather like Germany at the end of the Second World War, from the utter destruction of their cities started to grow the economic miracle that exists today. Unlike Germany, however, victory was not complete as the country remained divided.

The North Koreans felt they had won. Having stated from the beginning that it was South Korea who had started the war by launching an invasion across the 38th Parallel, they could claim they had successfully resisted aggression, defeated the United States and that its United Nations 'running dog lackeys' that they had retained control in their part of the country and could now, in the north, implement the socialist dream of classless freedom and labour emancipation.

In Baker Troop I am not sure if we knew whether we had won or not, but we knew we had not been defeated. Our minds were fully occupied in preparation for the move back to the new defensive positions on the Kansas Line.

CHAPTER ELEVEN

Baker Troop's Enemy

When Baker Troop landed in Korea we were given no briefing about the history of the Chinese soldiers, their motivation or morale. I had seen plenty of pictures of German soldiers in their grey uniforms and of German paratroopers with their smocks and round helmets and was very familiar with the S.S. skull and crossbones badge and high-peaked cap set at a jaunty angle. I knew how efficient the 88mm anti-aircraft gun had been against our tanks and what a frightening thing it had been to confront a Tiger tank with a bazooka. I had seen pictures of Japanese soldiers in their baggy uniforms and soft-peaked caps, carrying rifles with very long sinister-looking bayonets. But of the Chinese Army I knew nothing. In any war it is right, proper and understandable to paint the enemy in the blackest possible way. In describing the Chinese Army the common phrase used was that the People's Liberation Army (PLA) employed 'human wave' tactics, which implied a disregard for life, and that they attacked so ferociously because they were either drunk or high on drugs; they were mainly illiterate peasants and advanced in 'hordes' arming themselves by picking up the weapons of their fallen comrades. 'Hordes' was the term used for a long time and continued in press briefings until an American news reporter asked: 'How many hordes in a Division?'

There can be little doubt that the Chinese soldiers genuinely believed they were fighting against an evil Government which wished to invade their country and destroy their Government. Only two years before in 1949, the Communist Army had overthrown the Nationalist Government of General Chiang Kai Shek in a war that had begun in 1924. The epic endurance of the Long March, the continual war against Warlords, the Nationalists and the Japanese, had created an army used to hardship, used to going to war, used to suffering and used to victory. The reason for this success was not only the bravery and dedication of the soldiers but by continually and passionately broadcasting a message that appealed to the mass of ordinary people – in particular those living in rural areas – they obtained the support of the people. They proclaimed the doctrine that they were fighting not only to restore the ancient proud cultural heritage and traditions of the Han People but also to create an exciting unprecedented opportunity to break away from the existing class structure of serfdom, landlords and mandarins, to a system where they, the people, could live in freedom and prosperity and, very importantly, give an education to their children. They also appealed to hundreds of young patriotic men and women by fostering the image that the Red Army was genuinely fighting the Japanese to liberate China, as opposed to the Nationalists who were accused of compromise with the Japanese. It was a seductive and successful appeal, and hundreds of young students and workers who previously had no sympathy for communism joined the Red Army to fight the Japanese. From 1945 to 1949 victory followed victory and thousands of Nationalist soldiers, including whole Divisions with their officers, deserted Chiang Kai Shek and joined Mao. In spite of a flow of arms and ammunition continually being supplied to the Nationalists by the USA, the momentum of the Red Army could not be stopped and by September 1949 the whole of China was under communist control.

On 1 October 1949 Chairman Mao Tse Tung stood on a balcony in the Tienanmen Square, Peking, in front of a huge cheering crowd and declared the establishment of the People's Republic of China. It was a remarkable achievement. General Chiang Kai Shek and the remnants of his army had fled across the Straits of Formosa, and regardless of the wishes of the people of Formosa, established his Government in the island they renamed Taiwan.

How different it would have been if the United States had followed British Policy and recognised the defacto existence of the new Government in China. British policy did not mean they approved or disapproved of the new Government, but experience in dealing with a multitude of emerging new countries showed the wisdom of this recognition of reality. For the United States there was a choice;

many American diplomats and military representatives in Peking strongly advocated recognition of the Communist People's Republic, but in Washington there was the growing intensity of distrust and paranoia towards any regime that had an association with the word 'Socialist', or demonstrated an affinity with Communist Russia. There was also the significant impact made in Washington by the persuasive powers of the beautiful, articulate and extremely astute Madame Chiang Kai Shek, who argued effectively for continued recognition of the Nationalist Cause.

Before the Second World War the people of the United States had earned the respect and gratitude of the Chinese people by their generous, spontaneous and unconditional aid and support for education and religion. It was Britain that was tainted by imperialism and the memory of the Opium Wars. This feeling of warmth to the United States soon evaporated when Washington not only did not recognise the Chinese People's Republic and continued to give vocal support to Chiang Kai Shek but, as an overtly belligerent act, sent the 7th Fleet to the Straights of Formosa to prevent any invasion and made clear the retaliation and retribution that would be inflicted on China if any invasion was attempted. In New York at the United Nations the USA continually made speeches condemning the Peking Government, and so America became by definition an enemy of China.

We did not know that the Chinese Army was one of the most experienced armies in the world and had been continually in action for over twenty years. From 1924 the Chinese Communist Party had come to the conclusion that they would only achieve power by first politically defeating the ruling Party of Dr Sun Yat Sen, and then, militarily, the Nationalist Army of General Chiang Kai Shek. Although it instinctively felt a rapport with the Soviet Communist Party, Moscow had initially urged it to co-operate with the Nationalists, but as this had proved a disaster, and after many of the Communist Leaders had been betrayed and executed, the survivors fled and had begun the process of creating their own army. In October 1934 they undertook what has been described as the greatest physical feat in the twentieth century. Mao Tse Tung led 86,000 men and women through the encircling Nationalist Blockade, and by continually marching and changing direction, avoided defeat by the Nationalist Army of five million men that launched offensive after offensive to destroy them. They walked seventeen to twenty-four miles a day, crossed twenty-four rivers, seventeen provinces and eighteen mountain ranges. They experienced every sort of weather and hardship, and during the walk performed amazing acts of individual courage. The most famous episodes included the crossing of the Tatu River on a swaying bridge under a hail of enemy fire, making alliances with minority groups by drinking chicken blood, marching through inhospitable swamps without sufficient supplies, and promoting the revolutionary spirit in seemingly hopeless conditions.

The Long March is considered one of the great turning points in the history of the Chinese Communist Party and the Chinese Army. The March itself became legendary, and its survivors were treated with reverence and rewarded for the rest of their lives. By October 1935 they had reached the sanctuary of Shantung, having lost over 60,000 of their number. It was the men and women who shared and survived the suffering and traumatic experience of the Long March who bonded together for the rest of their lives with a remarkable sense of unity and determination to continue the fight, whatever the losses or consequences. They were hidden in the Shantung caves with virtually no weapons or supplies and with little chance of escape, and General Chiang Kai Shek was confident he would soon achieve their annihilation and began mobilising his armies to do this. Mao Tse Tung's survival tactic was to persuade the local peasant population to supply food, manpower and recruits by a mixture of ruthless killing of landlords, and preaching a new socialist doctrine of social emancipation. Soldiers worked in the fields, payment was made for supplies, and cadres opened schools and preached the difference between the 'oppressive Nationalist Government' and the new 'Revolutionary People's Army'. The poor were helped; landlords were killed.

In spite of their passionate belief in Socialism, it is probable that the miniscule People's Army would have been eventually defeated by Chiang Kai Shek, but in 1936 Japan, with its modern army, navy and air force, invaded China with a savage disregard for the lives of civilians and a ruthless indifference to the destruction of cities and the cruelty of their soldiers. As they drove deeper and deeper into China, General Chiang Kai Shek faced a dilemma; he had to stop the advance of the Japanese Army, but he himself was in no doubt that his main long-term enemy was the Communist People's Army. He therefore divided his forces and began fighting on two fronts. He launched attacks on the Japanese but simultaneously launched attacks on the Communists. It proved a fatal error. As stories of the terrible atrocities committed by the Japanese became more widespread, a spirit of revenge grew, especially among the young, and with it grew the public perception that Chiang Kai Shek was compromising with, and not fully committed to defeating, the Japanese. Mao Tse Tung grasped this opportunity and broadcast his famous call: 'Chinese should not fight Chinese, but a common enemy.'

It was a successful policy. Thousands of young men and women travelled to Shantung to join in the fight against the hated Japanese. Having always been forced to fight an enemy of superior numbers and fire power, the Red Army developed its own tactical doctrine: use rifles, machine guns and stick hand grenades. Attack at last light when the sun is shining in the eyes of the enemy, try to close in on a small isolated position, open an assault with as much artillery and mortar fire as possible and then, accompanied by the noise of whistles and bugles, attack a small area with superior numbers. At the same time, send other groups to infiltrate around the flanks of the enemy position to prevent its ability to launch a counter-attack, and then continue to attack, and attack until all the defenders had been killed or forced to withdraw.

Given the overwhelming power of the Nationalist bombers, their ground-strafing fighter aircraft and their own limited load-carrying capability, the Red Army quickly discovered the need to use convoys of people, not lorries, to carry forward supplies of food and ammunition, to avoid walking by day and to use every ingenious method to camouflage movement. Given the long distances to be covered and the lack of a logistic support, the soldiers also got used to carrying their own simple rations of rice and vegetables and their bedding roll on their back and, apart from medical support, not to expect any of the comforts considered essential by United Nations soldiers. All these lessons were used in the forthcoming war in Korea. As the Argylls reported after the battle at Kapyong: 'The quality of the Chinese Communist has now been accurately assessed, and it is realised that he is a tough and tenacious fighter of similar class to the Japanese, possessed of considerable skill in the handling of machine guns and mortars and well trained in night fighting. He can be expected to remain in his hill positions until prodded out with a bayonet and it is usual for him to do so. He is, in fact, a first class soldier, with whom you can take no chances.'

The Red Army as a matter of policy also avoided indiscriminate destruction. This was partly because they had limited artillery and air power, but also because they hoped to be occupying and restoring the destroyed cities and villages and did not want to antagonise the residents. In Korea, the Chinese were surprised by how freely the Americans would resort to what they considered excessive and unnecessary force. One Chinese soldier stated that if the Americans encountered a single sniper hiding in a house or village they would invariably call in massive artillery and air attacks, destroying the entire village and killing everyone in it. He asked: 'Why do they do this instead of simply sending soldiers in to kill the sniper?' This policy of using maximum force to prevent casualties is perhaps understandable and has been used subsequently in Iraq and Afghanistan. Tactically it certainly saves American lives, but as what are now called 'kinetic weapons' become more destructive and 'collateral damage' increases, strategic advantages may be lost.

The Red Army tactics of mass attacks on relatively small objectives brought success and this attracted more and more volunteers. Matching this military success was the equally important need to be successful in political indoctrination. It was not enough to defeat the enemy; it was even more important to inculcate into the minds of soldiers and civilians the belief in socialism and the need for political reform. It was a heady mixture and achieved an unimaginable result, and when on 1 October 1949 the Chairman announced the establishment of the People's Republic of China, he commanded an Army of five million men.

In the latter stages of their 'War of Liberation' thousands of Nationalist troops surrendered to the Communist forces and were absorbed into the People's Liberation Army (PLA). The task of the Communists was to convince these new soldiers that they were now in an army which worked on behalf of all the people and that a socialist regime was a joyful initiative allowing wonderful scope to develop a fresh and vibrant new China. The hierarchy of Mao Tse Tung's Party felt more comfortable with the socialist philosophy of the Soviet Union as opposed to the capitalist system in the West, but in 1950 did not see themselves as in any way subordinate to Moscow's wishes. Several times before the Second World War, when Soviet advisors had joined the Communist 'insurgents', significant differences had arisen as to the best way forward. Moscow favoured a concentration of effort on the urban population; Mao that success would result from recruiting the rural population. Mao won.

As the Communist forces were small and ill armed in comparison with the Nationalist Army which had been supplied with artillery and tanks by the USA, the secret of Communist success lay in convincing the population that theirs was a better system for China. This is why so much effort was made by the communist leadership and the PLA to walk'with two legs' in their approach to those who disagreed with them. The first tactic would be to have discussions with those who were'backward in their thoughts' to show them how wrong they were and to highlight the advantages of socialism. This was done by arranging for public meetings to be held in every village and urban district where anyone who previously held a senior position, or was rich, especially rich landlords, would be put on trial and the community would be pressurised and cajoled into making public criticisms. The guilty would then be paraded through the street wearing 'dunces' hats and embarrassing clothing. Given the size of the population, comparatively very few were executed, although many were sentenced to long terms of hard labour and their families were disgraced and impoverished. The policy was to demonstrate leniency; punishment was only applied if you were obstinate enough not to recognise and accept your own guilt.

In the PLA this system was used extensively. At every level of command, following the Soviet system, there was a political cadre appointed. Every day long meetings would be held where a point of communist doctrine would be put forward and then debated. This would be followed by a session of 'self-criticism' where each individual would be required to stand up and admit in detail their failings and errors of political judgement. The remainder of the group would then be required to attack the individual, to elaborate on his/her mistakes and to use all their skill to highlight false confessions and hypocrisy. It was terrifyingly successful and was a system that subsequently had significant implications in the way that the Chinese handled and dealt with UN prisoners, in particular American and British Commonwealth Prisoners.

It was this policy of trying to convert an enemy by persuasion rather than force that motivated many of the behaviours of the Chinese infantry. There was not the deep feeling of hatred that existed in the fight against the Japanese where the memories of the Rape of Nanking, the systematic slaying of soldiers and the slaughter of civilian populations led to an overwhelming desire for revenge. There are incidents recorded of prisoners being shot at the point of capture and those captured early in 1950 suffered terrible treatment from the North Koreans as they were marched North, but there are no cases of the Chinese Army lining up soldiers and shooting them, of herding civilians into a church and then burning the church, of public decapitations or mass hangings of women and children, all of which happened in the Second World War. The Chinese soldiers were prepared to fight ferociously and hard, but there was an element of humanity. Quoted in A.J. Barker's excellent book *Fortune Favours the Brave* is the story of how, in the Chinese attack on the Black Watch in November 1952, Corporal Wilson was wounded in the knee and watched as the Chinese moved around, regardless of their own safety, removing their dead and wounded: 'At the end, one Chinese came along and shook my hand saying in broken English, "Good Luck."' In the many accounts of those taken prisoner, the constant theme is to the effect that after being captured, despite the turmoil and confusion on the battlefield and the living standards of the Chinese: 'My wounds were tended and I was fed.' One badly wounded American was marched in a column north for two weeks with little or no medical care as there was none available. Then one night, to his surprise, the column was turned and marched south towards the American lines where he was left and subsequently rescued. Marches back to a prisoner of war camp were terrible; often in bitter weather with lack of food and in constant fear of Allied air attacks. They were reminiscent of the marches forced on prisoners of war at the end of the war in Europe when RAF prisoners were marched away from the advancing Russians or, at the end of the war with Japan, when prisoners were marched to death through the jungle, but in Korea there does not seem to have been a deliberate policy of causing additional hardship as a punishment.

The perception of brutality by the Chinese came from the way they treated their prisoners of war after their arrival in the prison camps. This was explained to new arrivals by the commandant of No. 1 Prison Camp on the Yalu: 'After capture, prisoners must be friendly and no longer adopt a hostile attitude. They must learn repentance and the meaning of peace. They are lucky to be alive after fighting for the capitalists and they should be grateful they are prisoners of the Chinese and have the chance to study until they go home. The lenient policy is unchangeable but there must be no sabotage of studies. A hostile attitude to study or any attempt to spoil other students' study will be punished. If you are friendly to us you will be treated as a friend, but the Lenient Policy has its limitations as regards our enemies.'

It was a policy quite different from any policy experienced by our prisoners of war before. It took a long time for the West to realise that the motivation of the captors was not to elicit information about units, tactics, weapons and future operations; it was to achieve a conversion to socialism. If you were prepared to co-operate and show genuine belief in the superiority of socialism over capitalism and were convinced of the illegality and wickedness of the Imperialists in their endeavour to occupy Korea, then there was a 'lenient policy'. If you were obstinate, uncooperative, ill-disciplined and rude, you had to be punished for your own good until you saw the light. The punishment was cruel, could be prolonged, and was designed to keep you for long periods in isolation in maximum uncomfortable circumstances. There is a similarity to the torture carried out during the period of the Spanish Inquisition where a conversion and confession of mistaken beliefs were necessary to avoid pain. The Inquisition tactics could, and did, take the form of continual physical beatings, amputations, burning and torture with instruments involving stretching the limbs. This is different from the Chinese process known as 'brain washing.' Beatings did take place, pain was inflicted, but the Political Cadres went to extraordinary lengths to avoid having to take this last step. They knew, as many of our bravest soldiers discovered, that resorting to violence was a defeat for their ideology. The paradoxical lesson was learned that if they resorted to violence they had lost, and the victim became strengthened in his resolve to resist. There was no subtlety about a beating. They also knew that after prolonged periods of incarceration in holes in the ground known as 'kennels', the men who suffered this terrible ordeal came out even more determined not to admit any guilt. Three men who endured this terrible punishment, but retained their dignity, were Captain Anthony Farrar-Hockley, Fusilier D.G. Kinne and the Reverend Sam J. Davies, Padre to the 1st Battalion Gloustershires. Rev. Davies was subjected to particular hostility as it was a fundamental tenet of the Communist creed to denigrate Christianity, referring to it as the 'opiate of the masses', and it would have been a great success if they had managed to get a priest to recant. The faith of Rev. Davies however, carried him through this ordeal and he remained a source of worry and inconvenience to the Chinese. In the hope of obtaining a conversion, the Chinese decided to segregate the officers from the sergeants and the sergeants from the rest of the soldiers; this tactic failed and in each category, regardless of rank, men emerged who obstinately would not cooperate. The stories of these men are both heart-warming and humbling; it leaves the thought: 'What would I have done?'

For the political staff of the prison camp, the failure to convert a prisoner to 'Socialism' was taken very seriously. It was seen to be a significant psychological and moral defeat and meant 'loss of face' not only of the cadre concerned, but also of the senior cadre and all the members of his staff. A series of 'self-criticism' meetings would be held where everyone would spitefully point out the faults of the guilty cadre and then make an abject apology for their own shortcomings. The inevitable result would be that the failed cadre would be disgraced, demoted, and under the policy of 'reform through labour', sent to work in a rural remote area of extreme poverty and the poorest of living conditions.

The 'lenient policy' did not apply, however, to prisoners caught escaping or trying to escape. In these cases the Chinese would use torture to extract information about the escape plans. One Gunner Officer who had helped three other prisoners to escape was subjected to horrendous treatment as the citation for his George Medal shows: 'To obtain the route and escape plans of the escape party Captain Gibbon was hung from a tree by a rope fastened round his wrists which were bound behind his back and subjected to beatings and kickings for many hours. In addition, he was threatened with a pistol and subjected to various other forms of ill-treatment. He withstood all this treatment so much that they considered that he obviously could not impart the information they required, as he did not know it. Captain Gibbon's conduct and courage during this time was an inspiration to all the others in the camp.' Other methods used included pushing bamboo slivers under the fingernails and 'water boarding' which is a form of suffocation by pouring water on a cloth placed over the victim's face. This was a punishment that Captain Farrar-Hockley had to endure, and after the war we called torture. In 2010 President Bush announced that it was not torture if used by Americans to gain information from suspected terrorists. I wonder what Anthony Farrar-Hockley would have thought about that?

In the early 1950s this policy of 'Cooperation means Leniency' was a major factor in the success of a few dedicated communists taking over the huge country of China. As time went on, however, Mao, like all dictators, became less and less tolerant of opposition. He instituted mass purges which killed thousands of his countrymen. He began the campaign 'Let all the Flowers Bloom' which was a call for anyone who disagreed with Peking's policy to come forward and voice their opinions. But when they had done this he then launched the 'Cultural Campaign' and the 'Anti-Corruption Campaign', and using the 'Little Red Book' as a guide for action, stimulated thousands of students to drag out, and try in public, anyone who had opposed the Government or anyone they thought might possibly oppose the Government. It was a slaughter of the innocents; hundreds were killed, thousands were transported to the country and vast quantities of priceless antiquities were destroyed. In the 'Ying and Yang', ebb and flow, of Chinese history it was probably a turning point when the period of total communist domination began to move slowly towards more individual freedom. The use of force is ultimately self-defeating.

But this theory of 'Cooperation means Leniency' did not apply to the North Koreans. It was well known that in the Second World War the most cruel prison guards came from Korea and in 1950 there was no concept of making any effort to try political indoctrination; brute force was the way to treat prisoners. In 1904 Korea had been conquered by Japan and in 1910 had been formally annexed as part of Japan. Following this annexation, Japan made every effort to replace the Korean culture with a Japanese culture. All official language was in Japanese and in schools the Korean language was banned. The population was treated with the utmost barbarity, and even those working in Japan were subjected to intense racial discrimination. Many Koreans were, however, recruited into the Japanese Army and their attitude to prisoners reflected the Japanese concept – that those who allowed themselves to be taken prisoner were cowards who were a disgrace to their Emperor and their uniform, and as such it was justified to treat them harshly.

One of the ironies of being a soldier is the attitude taken to enemy dead. When the excitement and tension of self-preservation has passed, a visit to former enemies' cemeteries does not generate a feeling of joy, rather a sense of sadness and identity. This is typified in the reflective and dignified reaction of servicemen of all nationalities when they visit El Alamein where there is a cluster of cemeteries of both Axis and Allied dead. What of Baker Troop's former enemies? Since the signing of the ceasefire on 25 July 1953, there has been great interest and many estimates made of the number of Chinese soldiers who were killed in the Korean War, and it is very interesting, therefore, that on 19 October 2010 – the 60th anniversary of the entry of China into the War – that an authoritative figure was at last published. The total was the result of an extensive research programme carried out by the Dandong University in the Chinese Province of Liaoning, who wished to commemorate 'The War to Resist American Aggression and aid Korea'. Since 1990, the Museum had been collecting casualty information by sending researchers to some 2,670 counties and districts in the Chinese mainland and verifying each identification reported by local civil administrative departments with all other available information. The total casualty figure of the Communist People's Volunteers (CPV) was 183,108 officers and soldiers, and this total included fighting personnel who were killed in action, died after being wounded and died from illness brought about by the war. In this museum at Dandong there is a now a Memorial Wall that depicts this number of 183,108 casualties, breaking it down to include the figures from each province, region and municipality. Mr Yin Jibu, the Museum's Deputy Curator, has stated: 'Although there could be new discoveries of the casualties in the future, there will be little room for substantial increase. However, our work seeking for the CPV's martyrs will continue, so that all future generations will remember the martyrs' contribution and sacrifice.'

According to the Official Chinese Military History, Chinese ground forces of the CPV entered the Korean Peninsula on 19 October 1950 'To defend their own territory and to help the Korean People's Army against Syngman Rhee and the multinational forces assembled in the name of the United Nations, and their first battle against a battalion of Syngman Rhee's troops took place on 25 October 1950.' After the ceasefire the Central Committee of China decided to commemorate the War every year on the latter date and at the Memorial Ceremony on 25 October 2010, Vice Chairman Xi Jinping called the Chinese action sixty years ago 'A great and just war for safeguarding peace and resisting aggression.' On the same day, a similar Remembrance Ceremony was held at the CPV Martyrs' cemetery in Hoechang County in North Korea, which was attended by a Senior Chinese Military Delegation. This Cemetery contains the graves of thousands of Chinese soldiers, including that of Mao An Ying who was Chairman Mao Tse Tung's eldest son.

Initially, I found the fact that the Chinese had created beautiful war cemeteries and built memorial walls commemorating those killed in the Korean War rather disconcerting. The Chinese soldiers came in 'waves' and were 'hordes', and were somehow alien. It is we who create beautiful cemeteries and build Memorial Walls with individual names, but with the passing of the years those who fought for the United Nations in Korea will have no difficulty in saluting the memory of the Chinese soldiers who gave their lives for their cause. Chinese hordes and human waves had become individuals.

Attack by 1st King's Regiment on the Warsaw Caves, 1953. (© David Rowlands)

Brian Parritt,
Hong Kong,
1954.

The 'Gully Gully' man
at Port Said who
boarded the *Empire
Pride* and produced
live chicks, doves and
rabbits from his shirt.

Korean boys doing what I did in 1940, 1944 and 1945.

Baker One gun pit.

Baker Two gun pit.

Baker Three
gun pit.

Baker Four gun pit,
the morning after
the Battle of the
Hook, showing
piles of empty
cartridge boxes. The
gun had fired
nearly 500 rounds
that night.

The Laundry Shop that was placed 'Out of Bounds' by Sergeant Major Wroot.

A visitor to our
gun site.

The Sergeants of Baker Troop.

The visit to the US Artillery 8 inch heavy guns called 'The Persuaders'.

Variable Time (V.T.) shells which burst in the air and were so effective against troops in the open.

A quick move by Baker Troop to support an attack by the Korean Division on our flank.

Sergeant Major Charlie Wroot and Sergeant Croydon Onyett on the left who later won the Military Medal.

At the ENSA Concert Party. When the garter was shown the cheers must have been heard in Pyongyang.

Lance Bombardier Alder, on the right, who was killed standing next to Baker One by a premature explosion.

The result of a premature explosion in 45 Field Battery.

Baker One on a Harassing Fire Mission.

Captain Bill Miller, Baker Troop Commander, with the Thai Battalion the week before he was killed.

Giving fire orders to the Baker Troop from the Thai Battalion after the death of Captain Bill Miller.

Two Koreans recruited by Sergeant Clifford Jackson DCM MM Intelligence Corps, who returned to North Korea clandestinely and acted as agents.

Lance Bombardier Giles in front of the Baker Troop OP before the Battle of the Hook with pristine sign and sandbags.

Baker Troop OP and OP Party after the Battle of the Hook. Myself, Gunner Page standing behind Lance Bombardier Giles on the right, and Gunner Lake kneeling, plus unknown Gunner holding mug. Signs and sandbags are no longer pristine.

Examining a mortar crater just behind Baker Troop OP which had just landed and wounded a Kingsman.

Trench leading to Baker Troop OP before the Battle of the Hook.

Same trench leading to Baker Troop OP after the Battle of the Hook.

Following the Battle of the Hook everyone seemed a little dazed.

Duke of Wellington's roll call after the Battle of the Hook.

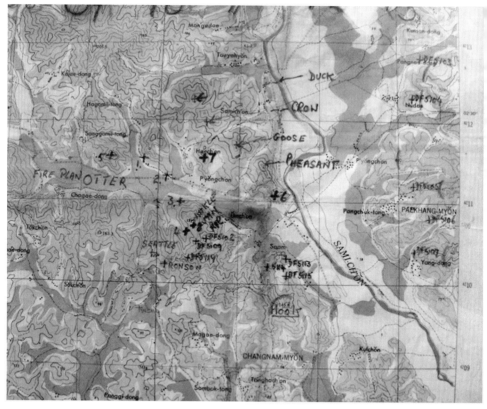

Photo of a map showing the Chinese positions and Artillery Fire Tasks carried in my pocket during the raid on the Warsaw Caves. A blood stain marks the spot after I was wounded.

Lieutenant Mervyn Ryder briefs members of his platoon who are going to provide two Standing Patrols outside our front wire that evening. They encountered the Chinese and three Kingsmen were wounded.

On the first day of the cease fire, Mervyn Ryder and I celebrated by sitting on top of Baker Troop OP.

Having 'illegally' left our front line and gone down into no-mans-land, we suddenly bumped into two Chinese solders, fortunately unarmed.

Baker Troop withdraws to the Kansa Line.

The Reception Centre at Panmunjom, waiting hopefully for the return of the prisoners.

A boisterous South African prisoner of war starts his journey home.

Baker Troop Mobile Command Post known as the 'Gin Palace' with the Chinese mortar round hanging in front.

Ladies in Seoul.

Girls in Seoul.

Baker Troop
says farewell to
those who were
not going home.

We board the *Empire
Pride* to return to
Hong Kong and are
checked by the
Swedish Neutral
Representative.

CHAPTER TWELVE

The Man Responsible for the War in Korea

In 1950 it was Kim Il Sung, commander in chief of the North Korean forces, who came to the conclusion that a military invasion of the south could destroy the South Korean Army, would force the Americans back to Japan and that thereafter, it would be very unlikely that America would launch a major seaborne invasion to regain Korea. The plan had military merit and it might well succeed if it had the approval of the Soviet and Chinese Governments; he began therefore to make preparations.

How was it then that the United States, with troops stationed in South Korea and an Army Command Headquarters in Japan, failed to perceive that this plan was not only being formulated, but there was a significant movement of troops, artillery and tanks up to the border to put it into practice? How was it that, in 1945, when the United States, in preparation for the defeat of Japan, had assembled the most sophisticated intelligence acquisition capability ever created, made such a bad mistake in 1950 in judging the likelihood of invasion by North Korea? Why was it that Washington continually told the commanders on the ground that an invasion was so highly improbable that measures were being taken to reduce the number of soldiers in Korea and that ships carrying ammunition to Korea were being diverted?

One fundamental reason for this grotesque misappreciation of North Korean intent and capability was the decision not to place Korea under the jurisdiction of General MacArthur who was their Commander of Far Eastern forces. Washington felt that General MacArthur had enough to do converting Japan into a democratic state and was apprehensive about his publicly stated view that Chiang Kai Shek should be supported in an invasion attempt to defeat the Communists which could lead to America being involved in a war with China. The decision was, therefore, that the American forces in Korea should be reduced to 500 'advisors' known as the Korea Military Assistant Group (KMAG), not under the command of General MacArthur, but reporting directly to Washington. Brigadier General Charles Willoughby, the Senior American Intelligence Officer in MacArthur's Far East Military Command, did not have any responsibility for the intelligence structure, tasking and analysis of intelligence emanating from Korea. This was the responsibility of the KMAG supported by the Central Intelligence Agency (CIA). Any intelligence produced in Korea went directly to Washington, was assessed, and then passed back to General Willoughby. It proved a fatal decision. Throughout the Second World War, General MacArthur had developed a great antipathy towards the Office of Strategic Services (OSS) (predecessor of the CIA); to such an extent that he had banned them from his theatre of operations. During the period leading up to June 1950, the CIA and the OSS were deeply engaged in an internecine struggle for supremacy which was not resolved until 1952 when the CIA were given responsibility for all clandestine and human source intelligence. This struggle of power between the OSS and the CIA added to the suspicion of MacArthur and Willoughby about the reliability of the KMAG assessments.

From 1945 to 1950 MacArthur had faced the enormous challenge of being the supreme commander in Japan and helping develop this ancient country from a military dictatorship steeped in the historical tradition of the Samurai with total loyalty to the Emperor, to a democratic and economically-successful country. That he had done this was a remarkable achievement. During the war, allied interrogators noticed a certain characteristic of the Japanese servicemen. In battle they would fight to the death and on many occasions committed suicide – 'Hara-kiri' – by pulling the pin from a grenade next to their chest or, in the case of an officer, disembowelling themselves with their sword rather than surrender. However, when captured, there was a remarkable change in attitude. The traditional 'soft man, hard man' tactic of questioning relied very little on the 'soft man'. The Japanese serviceman of any rank was trained to comply with orders and expected to be punished for mistakes. The interrogator would assume an aggressive attitude of authority and shout. Inevitably, the soldier would stand up to attention and reply 'Hai' – 'Yes' and would answer questions. Resistance to interrogation training was an inconceivable concept to the Japanese military.

Given this innate concept to obey a superior, it was a brilliant decision by MacArthur to allow the Emperor to retain his status and remain the focal point of authority and, just as General Tojo had actually been the man in charge during the Second Word War and made the decisions, so MacArthur was recognised to represent the Emperor and had to be obeyed. Then, by a combination of practical aid and cleverly crafted speeches which praised the Japanese people and avoided recriminations about past atrocities, he moved the nation towards establishing a new democracy. For MacArthur it was a most satisfying and enjoyable personal experience. It was, however, also a very time-consuming commitment, and reports of the possibility of an invasion by North Korea – an area not under his control – came very low on his time priority. When he did comment on the possibility of a North Korean invasion he made it clear that he felt it to be an unrealistic proposition and that, given the overwhelming power of the United States which had just won the war in Europe and the Far East, tiny North Korea would not risk certain annihilation by attacking the south. MacArthur prided himself on his knowledge of peoples he called 'Orientals'. He believed that 'Orientals' respected military strength and firm authoritarian leadership. It was a policy that may have worked in the Philippines and Japan but would fail when he tried to impose his will on the Chinese Communists.

Just as MacArthur believed it was not a credible proposition that North Korea would start a war, the same conclusion was reached by Washington but for a different reason. The conclusion of the Joints Chiefs of Staff, the American Intelligence Agencies and all the United States diplomats in Washington, was that North Korea was a loyal satellite of the Soviet Union and would never – could never – attempt military action without the agreement of Moscow, and they were comforted in this conclusion by the fact that the man in charge of North Korea was a totally dedicated supporter of Moscow.

Kim Il Sung, whom the Soviets had selected to be President of North Korea, had been a lifetime communist and his experiences of hardship and suffering for his beliefs had been very similar to Mao Tse Tung. At the age of seventeen he had joined the Chinese Communist Party and had been a founder member of the Communist Youth Group. He had taken up arms against the Japanese Army and by the age of twenty was an experienced guerrilla fighter in command of his own guerrilla band known as the Kapsan Group. From 1934 to 1940 he had fought the Japanese and became well known for his skill, bravery and powers of leadership, and his titles had changed from Battalion Commander to Divisional Commander, although, rather like titles in the IRA of the 1970s, the numbers involved did not compare to regular army numbers. Eventually, the Japanese made him their 'Most Wanted Guerrilla' and offered a reward of 200,000 Yen for his capture. Gradually, the pressure became too much and he fled to Russia and joined the Red Army where he became a captain and then commander of a special unit known as the 88th Special Sniper Brigade. This was a unit of around 200 Koreans who, like him, had also fled to Russia to escape the Japanese, or were ethnic Koreans who had grown up in Russia. The aim of the Soviets was not to use the 88th Brigade as a fighting unit but to use it as a force of political cadres. Like their Chinese counterparts, who shared the mutual experience of the Long March, members of the 88th Brigade formed a bond between themselves which combined patriotism with a dedication to communism. He was the ideal choice for the Soviets, therefore, when Russia was given control of all Korea north of the 38th Parallel and they had to find a president. When he returned to Pyongyang for the first time after the war he wore the uniform of a major in the Soviet Army.

In the south, the United States selected Syngman Rhee to be President. Before returning to Korea, Rhee – who had spent thirty-five years in the USA, obtained a Harvard degree and a PhD from Princeton – had become well known in political circles as the advocate for resistance against the Japanese and for Korean independence. He spoke fluent English, was a convert to Christianity, and his constant theme was to defeat Communism, unite Korea and foster the Christian religion. It was an attractive theme to the politicians in Washington, especially as he also had the support of General Chiang Kai Shek and the 'China Lobby'. Given the lack of knowledge about politicians in Korea and shortage of candidates for President, he was the natural choice and, as a sign of United States support and approval, he was flown to Seoul in Macarthur's own personal aircraft.

There was, however, a very big difference between the loyalty of Kim Il Sung to Russia and the loyalty and sense of obligation to the United States felt by Rhee. From the outset of his presidency he antagonised the American diplomats and commanders in Korea by his insistence on making a series of propaganda attacks against the north and continually taking actions along the border to provoke retaliation. Both Kim Il Sung and Rhee wanted the reunification of Korea but under their own respective jurisdictions. The difference was that the Soviet Union was sympathetic to the spread of communism and was prepared to take risks to achieve this aim to the extent that they provided Kim Il Sung with 150 T-34 tanks, hundreds of artillery pieces and a large number of aircraft. The United States wanted no part in provoking the north and was unsympathetic to the rhetoric of Rhee. American policy was to maintain the status quo; they had agreed the division of the country along the 38th Parallel and were very much against any action by Rhee that might upset this arrangement. Their stated policy was that the South Korean forces should be seen as a 'Constabulary' rather than an army and so, although they constantly made speeches of support for the Rhee Government, they deliberately withheld the supply of tanks, artillery and aircraft to the Republic of Korean forces. Many American officials, having seen the millions of dollars of military aid that had been given to Chiang Kai Shek, now in the possession of the Red Army, were reluctant to start sending more equipment to a Far Eastern country. Not surprisingly, this lack of commitment by the United States for reunification led to a lack of intelligence co-operation between the South Korean Intelligence Agencies and the Americans. More importantly, as Washington believed that Rhee was trying to dramatise and highlight the threat from the north in order to obtain more military supplies which might lead him to initiate an attack, as a matter of routine they denigrated and negated the intelligence reports coming from Seoul.

Washington was correct in its assessment that the Soviet Union did not want to risk a Third World War and that Stalin would not allow a situation to develop in North Korea, or any other country in their new Soviet Bloc, which might force them into a war with the United States. In 1949, nine months before the North Korean invasion, the Russians exploded their own atomic bomb and NATO and the Soviet Bloc had entered the age of mutual nuclear deterrence. What Washington did not foresee was that Kim Il Sung would be able to prepare a case which would convince Stalin that the north could invade the south and reunite the country without the public involvement of the Soviet Union and thus avoid a direct confrontation with the United States. It was this failure to anticipate such an eventuality that gave Washington the confidence to reject any intelligence reports they might receive of North Korean aggression. It also gave them the confidence to accept that there was no need to make any great effort to gain intelligence about North Korea. It was this erroneous confidence that both Washington and MacArthur shared that war was not a credible possibility that meant that North Korea was removed as an intelligence acquisition target, and any intelligence that did emerge was discounted. As to their main worry that Rhee might take matters into his own hands and start a war, they were comforted that on 24 June, the day before the invasion occurred, the United Nations Military Observers, who had carried out a field trip along the 38th Parallel, reported that: 'The South Korean Army is organised entirely for defence and is in no condition to carry out an attack on a large scale against the forces of the north.' They made no comment about the build up of the North Koreans and the imminence of the attack.

CHAPTER THIRTEEN

Why Did Baker Troop Go to War?

In the quest for why 20th Field Regiment and Baker Troop in particular went to Korea, the critical moment was in 1949 when General Omar Bradley, Chief of Staff of the American Army, ordered his Contingency Planning Staff in the Pentagon to prepare a paper of the actions to be taken in response to an invasion of South Korea. This was refined to include bringing in the United Nations 'If diplomacy failed.' In every military headquarters there will be a number of staff officers preparing plans for what are generally considered highly unlikely eventualities. It is not considered to be one of the best staff jobs, as it means a lot of work that never comes to fruition. Before writing the paper the planning staff would have requested an intelligence brief of the situation and been told the official assessment that an invasion by the north was highly unlikely and not a 'credible proposition'. This assessment was based on the assumption that an invasion would only happen if it was sanctioned by the Soviet Union, and this was an unrealistic proposition given the known wish of the Soviet Union not to start a Third World War. The Planning Staff would have also been told that the decision had been made to withdraw all combat units from South Korea and the policy for the remaining US forces in the KMAG was to assist in the training and reorganisation of the South Korean Army. They would also be aware that decisions had been made to withdraw combat units from Japan, reduce the number of regiments in the remaining divisions and rotate home the great majority of soldiers who had combat experience. They would also know that because Washington did not regard Korea as a potential military problem but was seen as a political problem that Korea had been removed from the jurisdiction of MacArthur, the Commander Far East. The result was that the Washington-based Contingency Planning Team did not involve the staff in Tokyo in their plan of action in the case of a North Korean invasion; a very bad mistake given the inevitable involvement of the US forces in Japan in the event of an invasion so close to Japan.

As a result, therefore, whereas as a matter of routine a contingency plan will designate units to be involved, command structures to be established, timings to be suggested and logistic support required, in this case the plan had to be very speculative and ambiguous. The dramatically significant point, however, which ultimately had a direct effect on Baker Troop, was the statement that: 'If diplomacy failed then the United Nations should be requested to provide a military force', and this statement they added to their conclusions. It must have been a most satisfactory conclusion for the staff officers concerned; their paper could finish on a positive note and no one felt there was a need to explain how this unprecedented United Nations force could actually be raised, organised or commanded, and there were certainly no planning staff in the United Nations with whom they could discuss such details. Anyway, there was no need to do this, as an invasion was not a 'credible proposition'; they had done their job and the paper could be put in the filing cabinet along with other academic exercises. It is no surprise, therefore, that when the invasion did occur, the contingency plan had no military value whatsoever and was a waste of time.

On 25 October 1950 the incredible happened and the North Korean army swarmed over the border. President Truman was at home in Independence, Missouri, and Mr Dean Acheson, his Secretary of State, was on his farm in Maryland. They flew back to Washington and together with their senior diplomatic and military advisors discussed what to do. The general view was that this was part of a Soviet-inspired plot to extend communism in the Far East and that weakness in American response would act as a catalyst for further invasions. Two major decisions were made immediately; first to send MacArthur to Korea to get his appreciation of the situation and obtain his recommendations, and second to send the 7th Fleet to the Straits of Formosa. The given story was that the movement of the

7th Fleet was to prevent a retaliatory invasion by China of Taiwan, although this was not a military possibility; Red China had already tried to do this once and had been heavily defeated. The actual reason was to prevent any military initiative from Chiang Kai Shek. Early on the morning of 30 June the report from MacArthur arrived and was the catalyst for the start of the war. It read: 'The only assurance for holding the present line and the ability to regain the lost ground is through the introduction of US ground forces into the Korean battle area. To continue to utilise the forces of our Air and Navy without an effective ground element cannot be decisive.'

President Truman was called at 0500 hrs on 30 June, agreed with the assessment of MacArthur, and made the fateful decision to approve the sending of ground forces to Korea. MacArthur had felt that two divisions would be sufficient and this was also agreed.

It would be nice to think that this decision was an altruistic decision based on the wish to liberate the South Korean people, but this would be a naïve assumption. Truman, as a Democrat, had won the election to be President on his own personality and not as before because he was Vice President. When President Roosevelt died, the Republican opposition was determined to defeat him at the next election and had chosen as their most powerful argument the failure of the Democrats to give adequate support to General Chiang Kai Shek. There was a very powerful 'China Lobby' pressing for more support for Taiwan and there was a powerful 'Military Lobby' pressing for increased defence expenditure to confront the growing threat from the Soviet Union. When Truman led America into the war it was with the agreement of the House of Representatives and the Senate; everyone regretted going to war, but there was universal agreement that it was in America's strategic defence interest to do so. It was very satisfying, therefore, that this naked nationalistic objective could be wrapped in the embrace of the United Nations and projected as a war against aggression.

In the days between the invasion and Truman's decision to send ground troops to Korea, the 1949 Contingency Plan had been pulled from the filing cabinet with its conclusion that in the event of an invasion, 'If diplomacy failed', the response should be the formation of a United Nations Military Force. Taking advantage of the fact that the Soviet Union was boycotting the Security Council, because it disagreed with the decision not to allow Red China to fill the Chinese seat on the Security Council, the United States submitted a Resolution asking for United Nations approval for the creation and use of such a United Nations Military Force to support South Korea, with the aim of defeating the North Korean Army and establishing a United Korea. On 27 June, two days after the invasion, this Resolution was approved with only two abstentions – India and Egypt. The critical statement that 'If diplomacy failed' was accepted as being the de facto situation; diplomacy had cleared failed because the invasion had taken place. Britain had now joined in a war where its only role had been to sit, watch and nod its head as the United States came to the conclusion that ground forces should be deployed, that this force should comprise two divisions from Japan, and that General MacArthur would become commander of a United Nations Force.

It was to be in compliance with this resolution to support a United Nations Force that on 19 August Brigadier Coad was told he was to take his brigade to Korea and on 28 August two battalions; the Middlesex Regiment and the Argyll and Sutherlands Highlanders, plus an Infantry Workshop and an Ordnance Field Park, arrived in Pusan. They had no clear mission, no heavy weapons, no armoured support and no logistic training to fight a modern, well-equipped, highly motivated and victorious enemy. The British Government had bolstered its diplomatic influence with a total disregard for the required military capability. It was the first example, repeated later, where British politicians acquiesced to American pressure for cooperation in a war where, as the United States provided the overwhelming number of troops, aeroplanes and ships, they automatically provided the command element and Washington made the strategic decisions. It was a war that led to the commitment of twenty-two countries to send military forces to a war, far from their shores and posing no immediate threat to their sovereignty and which led to the deaths of over two million people. The condition that military force should only be used 'If diplomacy failed' was not relevant because diplomacy had not been used to prevent the war. It was the failure of the United States to recognise that North Korea might invade the south and saw no necessity, therefore, to make any diplomatic initiatives either to Stalin, Mao Tse Tung or Kim Il Sung, to make it clear that such an invasion would result in a devastating United States response that allowed Kim Il Sung to persuade Stalin that an invasion could be successful. For the gunners of Baker Troop, however, issues such as internecine political pressures in the United States, conflicts of interest between General MacArthur and the CIA, machinations behind the scenes at the United Nations and fears of Soviet expansion were irrelevant. The North Koreans had invaded the south and the British Government had agreed with the United Nations Resolution that the South Korean people should be liberated. It was a worthwhile thing to do.

CHAPTER FOURTEEN

What Intelligence Was Available Before the Invasion by North Korea?

Traditionally, intelligence about another country's military capabilities and intentions comes from diplomatic sources within the country, signals intelligence, photographic intelligence and agents. By June 1950, none of these traditional methods were targeted on the threat from North Korea. United States and United Kingdom diplomatic representation in North Korea did not exist, and discussions with diplomats who were allowed into North Korea confirmed the intention of North Korea, like South Korea, to 'reunify Korea', but this was judged to be an aspiration rather than an intention to go to war. Because America refused to recognise the Government of Mao Tse Tung, there was no United States diplomatic representation in Peking and the Indian Ambassador was used as an intermediary. Signals Intelligence, perhaps the most important indicator, was painfully inadequate. The reason being that Korean Signal Intelligence was seen to be a sideshow to the main target which, since the late 1940s, had been the Soviet Union. Up to 1948, Britain and America had been reading many of the codes of the USSR, then, suddenly in the space of one day, 28 October 1948, this ability virtually disappeared. The Soviet Union abruptly and radically changed its codes, ciphers, procedures and equipments, and Britain and America were suddenly 'electronically blind'. The reason for this change in Soviet security was probably information provided by a spy called William Weisband who had been born in the USSR, lived in the United States, had been a

KGB agent since 1932 and since 1942 had worked in the US code-breaking department where he remained undiscovered until in May 1950. Other spies who may have revealed the fact that the allies were reading Soviet traffic include Klaus Fuchs and the members of the 'Famous Cambridge Five' who were recruited during the Second World War by the Russian Agent Arnold Deutsch – Guy Burgess, Donald Maclean, Kim Philby and Anthony Blunt. The alleged 'fifth man' became the focus for intense Security Service and media interest for many years, and allegations were made about Sir Roger Hollis, former Head of MI5; Victor Rothschild 3rd Baron Rothschild, and the ex-Government Minister Goronwy Rees, but to this day no conclusive evidence has been produced as to his identity. There was also a man called John Cairncross who worked at Bletchley Park and who admitted 'feeding stuff to the Russians on a weekly basis.' Whoever it was that convinced the initially disbelieving Russians that their expensive and complicated communication systems had been penetrated and were not secure is not certain, but when convinced they acted immediately and changed everything. For the allies, therefore, 28 October 1948 became 'Black Friday' and this had a significant effect on the Signals Interceptions capability to read Korean traffic.

Another major factor for the lack of signals intelligence concerning Korea was the difference of opinion between the United States and the United Kingdom regarding the recognition of the new Peking Government. America stood by Chiang Kai Shek and put its 7th Fleet in the Straights of Formosa to prevent an invasion. Britain, however, adopted the opposite policy and, in the United Nations, publicly recognised the new Communist State of Mao Tse Tung. In the Second World War, Britain and the United States had signed a significant agreement to share intelligence and avoid duplication relating to Signals Interception. This was a far-reaching agreement that is still secret and extant, and often comes under the controversial description of 'The Special Relationship'. In 1949, however, the United States, which considered that under the Potsdam Agreement Korea was under its jurisdiction, declined to share signals intelligence on the basis of 'the political differences between us over China'.

Another factor was that about this time the North Koreans, like the Soviets, made strenuous efforts to improve their communication security. Supported with technical advice from the Soviet Union, they became scrupulous about radio silence with most traffic being sent by landline and undersea cables effectively cutting off access to their conversations. There was also extensive use of 'One Time Pads'. As a result of all these factors, prior to June 1950 there was virtually no signal Intelligence coverage of North Korea and when North Korean traffic was recorded, and it was confirmed that it came from a Non-Soviet source, as an act of policy, the coverage was dropped and what little North Korean radio traffic was inadvertently intercepted as a result of listening to Soviet Nets was not analysed. In April 1950 two positions to intercept North Korean communications were set up as a 'Research and Development Study' and approximately 200 messages became available for analysis, but by the time of the invasion on 25 June 1950, none of these messages had been processed. Analysis of Soviet communications in 1950 did show an increase of interest in the Korean Peninsular and there was an interception that revealed a large shipment of bandages from the Soviet Union and Manchuria to North Korea, but these indications were only seen as significant in hindsight, after the invasion in June.

Before the invasion by North Korea the capability to read Korean voice traffic had been non-existent. The US National Security Agency (NSA) responsible for radio interception had no Korean dictionary, no Korean-speaking or reading staff and, very importantly, no Korean typewriters. Eventually, two extremely elderly ex-teachers were found to help, but these gentlemen had no military experience and no security clearances. There was also a shortage of radio operators who could take down Chinese Morse, which had fifteen extra letters. In 1952, although a large number of National Servicemen were selected to learn Russian Morse, only two young Royal Signals soldiers, one of whom was Signalman Michael Stubbings, were selected to go to the Wireless Troop at Mansfield Woodhouse for a six-month crash course to learn Chinese Morse. After completion of the course the two sailed on the *Empire Pride* to Kure and then, to their surprise, were posted to the American aircraft carrier, the USS *Boxer*. Here they worked on twelve-hour shifts for four months listening on US AR 88 sets until American replacements arrived. Reception was weak and although Russian Morse arrived at over thirty words a minute, and the Chinese speed was only eighteen, unlike Russian morse where an experienced listening operator could eventually pick up the idiosyncrasies of an individual sender and recognise his style, there was no way of identifying the Chinese operator. The two soldiers were amazed at the variety of food on board the ship. Having just come from the rationing in England they revelled in the availability of steaks and ice cream. As they had no way of getting money on board, their senior officer asked how much they earned a week and, on being told it was seven shillings and sixpence a day, he gave them twenty dollars a week for expenses which they spent mainly on Hershey chocolate bars. They did get opportunities to visit the flight deck and watched the Corsair planes take off and land. It was a most unusual posting for British Army soldiers and perhaps it is possible that they qualified for an American Korean Naval Medal.

Although in 1950 the capability to read North Korean signal traffic was virtually non-existent, the United States signals community has always demonstrated a remarkable ability to adapt to new requirements and by 1953 this challenge had been met.

The standard procedure to handle intelligence is known as the Intelligence Cycle; first information is collected, then collated, analysed, turned into intelligence and then disseminated to those who need it. Before this cycle is put into motion, however, there is a major decision to be made – what is the target? In early 1950 the strategic decision was made that there was no need to collect information/intelligence about North Korea. Both Washington and General Macarthur agreed on this point; the result was that just as there was a positive decision not to divert resources to listen to North Korean radio traffic, there was a firm decision that there was no need for aerial photographic cover of North Korea. Much attention was paid to military movement in the Russian Port of Vladivostok and 'Top Secret' high-altitude photographic flights were authorised over Russia, but no aerial coverage was undertaken of the build up of North Korean forces on the 38th Parallel. Thus, two of the most important sources of information, Signal Intelligence and

Photographic Intelligence were not targeted against what proved to be the major threat.

The last significant source of intelligence in peacetime is the reporting by agents and sources. 'Our Man' in Seoul was George Blake who had a tiny staff and who, because of the political differences with the United States, had very few liaison contacts. He was sent to Seoul in 1948 to target north-east China and the Communists in Korea, but given the difficulty of recruiting agents in the North, it is not surprising that those he did recruit were later described as 'venal'. He was probably more interested in trying to provide intelligence about the ever-changing political situation in South Korea, which was causing great concern in London.

In 1949 George Blake made a contribution to the Korean Assessment produced by the Joint Intelligence Committee (JIC), which is the most senior Intelligence Committee in the United Kingdom, and which stated that the number of North Korean troops available for an invasion into the South was 36,000. General MacArthur, sitting in Japan, made his assessment that the number of North Korean troops was 136,000 but did not feel they posed a threat. It was a huge difference, but a year later British Military Intelligence was still refusing to accept American estimates, arguing that they were 'infected by MacArthuritis.' George Blake was subsequently captured by the North Koreans and became a Soviet spy, betraying up to 400 of his colleagues. He was arrested in 1960 and sentenced to forty-two years imprisonment but, in very unusual circumstances, managed to escape from Wormwood Scrubs – a high-security prison – and successfully reached the Soviet Union. Given the gross mistakes made in his estimates of North Korean troops available to invade the south, there was a subsequent suspicion that his conversion to Russian Socialism had taken place before his capture. This suspicion was increased when it became known that in Russia he was awarded the Order of the Patriotic War 1st Class, the Order of the Honoured Employee of the Russian Federation of the Foreign Intelligence Service, the Order of Lenin, the Order of the Red Banner, the Order of Friendship and the Order for Personal Courage. In 2011, aged eighty-eight, he was still living in Moscow with his second wife and son.

In August 1949 the Soviet Union, to the surprise of the West, had detonated an atomic bomb; they had been able to do this by obtaining technical data from a sophisticated network of spies and agents. George Blake was a traitor, but there was also a spy living in London who, unknowingly, I invited to our wedding in 1956. Konon Molody, alias Gordon Lonsdale, was a Russian who had served as a gunner officer in the Second World War. He had then volunteered to do a long English language course and by a process of elimination was eventually selected to go to England and become the 'handler' for the traitors in the 'Portland Spy Ring'. The scenario for this wedding invitation was the coffee room of the School of Oriental Languages, a Department of London University in Tavistock Square. After 20th Field Regiment left Korea, we returned first to Hong Kong and then to the famous gunner barracks at Woolwich, just south of London. During this period an invitation came on regimental orders for volunteers to learn foreign languages and, for a combination of reasons, I decided to volunteer. To my surprise I was accepted to undergo a three-year period of tuition in Mandarin Chinese which meant one year in the School of Oriental Studies, followed by two years at Hong Kong University. I was delighted with this news; it would fulfil an ambition to go to university and it would enable me to discover more about the Far East, an area I found fascinating. The course started in September 1955, and the students were four soldiers to learn Mandarin, four to learn Cantonese, and two airmen and a sailor. We also had several young diplomats from Canada, Australia and the UK. There was also one civilian, a man who claimed he was Canadian but had lived most of his life in America. In retrospect it became clear that when he was with the Canadian diplomats he emphasised that his knowledge of Canada was limited, as he had lived in the USA. When questioned about life in America he emphasised his Canadian background. We never met outside the environments of the university, but one day, sitting together having coffee, I asked him why he was spending so much of his own money learning Chinese. He replied: 'Well, I am a businessman. There are 500 million Chinese; I sell those guys one trouser button each and that is 500 million trouser buttons.' I was impressed. The week before I had proposed to Pam, and we were busy arranging our wedding in

Lincoln before going to Hong Kong so, on the spur of the moment, I asked if he would like to join us. Thankfully he declined saying that he had to set up his new business. Later, when I applied to transfer to the Intelligence Corps and the subject of Lonsdale was raised, I was very glad he had declined. We would have called Lonsdale an agent if he had worked for us, but of course he was a Russian Spy as he worked against us. He was very successful both as a businessman and a spy. He set up a trade buying and renting jukeboxes and bubble-gum machines which were all the rage at the time, and, as a spy, he successfully collected secrets from Harry Houghton and Ethel Gee, the traitors who worked in the Admiralty Under Water Weapons Establishment, and Morris and Lona Cohen who worked under the Alias of 'Mr and Mrs Kruger'. Lonsdale was arrested and sentenced to twenty-five years' imprisonment but was released in exchange for the businessman Greville Wynne. I always had a sneaking admiration for Lonsdale. Many of my friends who studied foreign languages found themselves involved in espionage duties and did very well in this complicated profession; Lonsdale (Molody) did his job and in his memoirs was particularly pleased that as a socialist he had made a lot of money selling jukeboxes to the capitalists.

CHAPTER FIFTEEN

A North Korean Invasion of the South is not a Credible Proposition

Certain reports from the CIA did express concern about the dangers of Korean military intentions. A clandestine unit had been set up to recruit former Korean soldiers who had been in the Japanese Army and then to infiltrate them back to become government officials and soldiers in the North Korean Army. These men were reporting a build-up of forces and the development of communication facilities along the border. In the first half of 1950 a large number of other intelligence facts pointed towards the likelihood of an invasion led by Kim Il Sung with the tacit support of the Soviet Union and China. These included:

- International diplomatic sources reporting preparation by the North Korean forces for an invasion and an increase in the influence of Kim Il Sung in Moscow.
- Reports from the South Korean Government that there was an increasing danger of an invasion.
- Reports of significant military supplies and weapons being sent by the Soviet Union to North Korea.
- Reports of major construction works by the North Koreans to improve the roads leading to the border.
- Declaration of a Restricted Zone along the border by the North Koreans except for military transport.
- Removal of civilians from the border area.
- Recall of senior Soviet officials in North Korea back to Moscow (a move that was long recognised as a classic indicator of expected military action).

• Significant increase in North Korean propaganda broadcasts warning that the South Koreans were planning to attack the North.

With hindsight this collection of facts and indicators give ample warning that something was going to happen and it would be wise to take precautions, but none were taken. In Washington the accepted fact remained that the Soviet Union was not going to risk the outbreak of a Third World War by giving Kim Il Sung permission to begin military operation which would involve the United States. In Tokyo, MacArthur and his staff also accepted this premise and also remained confident in their view that it was unthinkable that North Korea would actually attack the most powerful Navy, Army and Air Force in the world.

The facts show that there were enough indications to give warning that an invasion of the south by North Korea was a distinct possibility, but because this did not match the perceptions of Washington and Macarthur, no intelligence acquisition systems were targeted against North Korea to confirm or discount these indications, and any intelligence that did suggest an invasion was deliberately discounted. If this myopic and grossly incorrect judgement had not been made, and if clear and positive statements had been made by Washington that an invasion of the south would be considered as an act of war against the United States, and it had reinforced troop levels in Korea, rather than reducing troop levels, it is highly likely that Moscow would not have given its practical but tacit support to Kim Il Sung. He would have been deterred from believing that a sudden and powerful invasion with his superior and better trained army would be able to conquer the south and leave him in control of the whole of the Peninsula without any international interference.

When mistakes occur it is correct to attribute responsibility to the senior person involved. It would be facile, however, to blame Truman and MacArthur individually for these two gross errors of judgement. By 1950 the Soviet Union had taken control over vast areas of Europe including East Germany, Poland, Czechoslovakia, Hungary, Rumania, Bulgaria, and Estonia, and had consolidated their control over the Soviet satellites including Ukraine. In 1949 the Berlin Blockade had been broken, at great cost, which had thwarted the Soviet intention of forcing the Allies to give up their sectors because of the threat of starvation and lack of energy. The Cold War was at its height and Truman was facing an aggressive Soviet Union determined to expand its influence over the rest of Europe. At home there were economic problems. Following the Depression of the late 1930s, in 1941 industrial output had surged to support a dramatically increasing war machine; by 1950 the impetus for this industrial expansion was declining and there was a need to reorient the American Industry towards a peacetime economy. There were a lot more pressing problems facing the White House than the Korean Peninsular, especially when your diplomatic staff and chiefs of staff agreed there was no need to worry.

For MacArthur, now aged seventy-two and sitting as supreme commander in Tokyo, the situation in Korea was not a great worry. He had had a brilliant war. After being ejected from the Philippines and fleeing in a small PT boat to Australia, he had commanded the Allied Forces in a series of strategic battles that step by step had destroyed the Japanese forces in the Far East. Throughout the Pacific conflict he had deeply resented the agreed Allied Policy that the liberation of Europe should be Priority One and the war in the Pacific, Priority Two, but this decision made him even more determined to succeed, regardless of what Washington, London or Moscow were saying. By 1945 MacArthur could legitimately claim that it had been his strategic plan of bypassing and isolating those islands that the Japanese had fortified and heavily manned, and then ferociously attacking less well-defended islands that had been successful. His strategy had always been the same; initiate a preliminary series of attacks at various diversionary points intended to conceal where the main attack was to take place; select a point well to the rear of the enemies' existing front line which was a critical point in their supply line and devastate this island with the heaviest possible aerial and sea bombardment, then land marines and immediately construct new airfields. It was a successful strategy; the initiative was torn from the Japanese who found themselves desperately trying to reinforce and supply their bypassed garrisons and never certain where the next landing would take place. Compared to the Middle Eastern, Italian and European campaigns, his geographic, climactic and logistical problems were far more severe, and he was constantly being told that the risks he was taking were too great. It was indeed a personal achievement that MacArthur led the Allied Forces to victory. He had been prepared for bloody battles in Japan itself and had formulated a terrifying sequence of aerial bombing which fortunately was not in the end required by the dropping of the two atomic bombs.

Having won the military battle against Japan, MacArthur's political achievement in Japan was just as significant. He landed, virtually alone and unarmed, and within weeks had achieved the successful co-operation of a defeated but proud people and army. Men, who had been willing to kill themselves, rather than surrender a short time before, now believed that it was the Emperor's will that they stayed alive and helped reconstruct their country. A thousand years of Bushido was changed. It was a remarkable achievement and great credit must be given to MacArthur who, in his moment of military triumph, used his position not for self-aggrandisement to humiliate the Emperor and thus provoke a visceral hostile reaction from the Japanese people, but to obtain their cooperation in what must have been for the Emperor an unimaginable mortifying position.

By June 1950 the 'democratisation' of Japan was moving steadily ahead, and in terms of any possible military threat Macarthur's main concern was the possibility of Soviet intervention into Japan. He believed that the Soviet Union was planning the global expansion of communism and that this expansion was targeted at the Far East rather than Europe. His stated aim was therefore to recruit a Japanese Defence Force that, in the event of any Russian invasion, could be used to augment the American forces based in Japan until reserves could arrive from the USA. Given that at the time of the North Korean invasion Macarthur had no responsibility for the Korean Peninsular, it was an immense change in his responsibilities when he was abruptly appointed to be commander in chief of the United Nations Forces and directed 'to restore peace, order and unity to the entire Korean Peninsula.'

On receiving the order that he was to take command, MacArthur did what he had done many times before in the Second World War; he flew to take a look at the situation himself. He landed at Sinwon when it was under aerial attack and saw the South Korean Army in full flight. It was a desperate situation; he had been put in charge of a defeated army retreating as fast as it could facing a victorious army, better armed, better organised and numerically superior. How could he overcome these great odds?

General Charles Willoughby has described his dilemma:

> How could he accomplish this when in fact nothing stood in the way of the enemy's tank columns rushing straight down the road from Seoul to Pusan? He reflected on Japan, which was his primary responsibility to secure and protect; how could he denude this great bastion of troops without inviting Soviet entry from the north? Could he find the transportation to carry the troops to the area and the munitions and supplies to sustain them in combat? Could he rally, reorganise and reinspire the defeated South Korean Army? Could he, if all this was accomplished and the enemy's tenuous supply lines extended to dangerous limits, cut these lines and then envelop and destroy his main forces with only a handful of troops available? First and foremost he must delay and impede the enemy's headlong rush. He had four scattered, woefully under-strength Divisions and one battalion of Australians.

With the agreement of Truman he decided to send reinforcements, and on 1 July the first elements of 24th Division reached Korea and, although outnumbered one hundred-to-one, set up roadblocks and tried to stop the North Korean advance. In the hand-to-hand fighting, the commander of 24 Division, Major General William Dean, who in 1944 had commanded a division in Germany, was surrounded and personally led several 'tank killer' teams, finally destroying a T-34 tank with a hand grenade. The general evaded capture for a month by hiding during the day and moving at night, but was eventually captured and became the most senior United Nations Prisoner of War. Although he was in prison for three years and subjected to long periods of intense interrogation and indoctrination, he never co-operated or capitulated. Truman awarded him the highest United States decoration, the Medal of Honor.

In the next weeks MacArthur rushed troops including Brigadier

Coad who had arrived with his two battalions, the Argyll and Sutherland Highlanders, and the Middlesex Regiment, from Japan to help man the perimeter. It was indeed a desperate situation and talk of a 'Pusan Dunkirk' circulated. The American Air Force with total air supremacy bombed and strafed the supply routes, but in spite of this air superiority the North Koreans were able to move at least two fresh divisions and two tank brigades from North Korea to the Naktong River on the Pusan perimeter. MacArthur now considered how he could use his amphibious capability to repeat his successes against the Japanese and cut the North Korean lines of supply. Because of the mountainous terrain, the main supply routes came down the west coast converging around Seoul. He decided, therefore, this was where to attack. The port he chose was Inchon. It was his own decision. Washington thought it far too hazardous and made objections about the supply of ships and the release of more Marine units; his own staff gave him a detailed list of the dangers of landing at Inchon ranging from the dominance of the city overlooking the inland harbour, the fear of mining and the navigational and tidal hazards. MacArthur heard all the dangers but felt that the only way to defeat the North Koreans was to 'throttle their supply lines.' He therefore ordered the operation to go ahead and landed the 1st Marine Division. At the same time he ordered a breakout from the perimeter. It was his classical 'two-pronged attack' and it was successful. The North Korean Army fell back in retreat across the 38th Parallel and Seoul was liberated. It was a great victory.

MacArthur re-enacted his triumphal re-entry into the Philippines and personally escorted President Rhee back into his battered capital. Here he made the significant statement that 'there is now the opportunity to establish a United Korea.' Praise was heaped on him. Truman wrote: 'I speak for the entire American people when I send you my warmest congratulations on the victory achieved under your leadership. Few operations in military history can match either the delaying actions where you traded space for time, or the brilliant makeover which has now resulted in the liberation of Seoul.' The American Joint Chiefs of Staff wrote: 'The JCS are proud of the great successes you have achieved. They would have been impossible without brilliant and audacious leadership. From the sudden initiation of hostilities you have exploited to the utmost all capabilities and opportunities. Your transition from the defensive to offensive operations was magnificently planned, timed and executed.'The British Chiefs of Staff wrote:'We have admired not only the skill which you have conducted an extremely difficult rear-guard action against the greatest odds over many anxious weeks, but equally the bravery and tenacity with which the forces under your command have responded to your inspiring and indefatigable leadership. We believe that the brilliant conceptions and masterly execution of the Inchon attack counter-stroke which you planned and launched while holding the enemy at bay in the south will rank amongst the finest strategic achievements in military history.'

It is perhaps ironic that seven months later when MacArthur was ignominiously sacked, the personal qualities which had given him the confidence to override so many objections and launch the Inchon attack and were so praised, now changed and he was described as arrogant, self-opinionated, god-like, disrespectful and 'too big for his breeches'.

While in Seoul, MacArthur summoned the North Korean Commander and issued an 'unconditional surrender ultimatum' which included the injunction to liberate all UN Prisoners of War and civilian internees, and make adequate provisions for their protection and care. He also made strict conditions about the surrender of the North Korean Army, the laying down of arms; the recognition of the South Korean Government and the acceptance of defeat.

There are many historians who feel that the Allied decision in the Second World War to continue the war until the Germans accepted the demand of 'unconditional surrender', did, in fact, prolong the war unnecessarily which resulted in more Allied casualties and made little difference to the eventual outcome. The Seoul ultimatum issued by a very confident General McArthur would have been seen by him as the next logical step in the process of fulfilling his military mission of defeating communism. It reflects his firm conviction that victory was going to be secured by force of arms, and not by diplomacy or negotiation.

The historian might say that as the war finished along the 38th parallel that General MacArthur's insistence on continuing the fighting did prolong the war, did result in more casualties and made little difference to the eventual outcome.

CHAPTER SIXTEEN

The Crossing of the 38th Parallel

The next major step was whether the United Nations forces should cross the 38th Parallel and occupy North Korea. MacArthur felt that this was necessary as, in order to fulfil his orders to restore a safe and secure South Korea, it was pointless to stop at an arbitrary line and allow the north the opportunity to regroup, rearm, and then launch another invasion at a time of their choice. Britain basically agreed with this move and on 25 September, Ernest Bevin, the Foreign Secretary, addressed the United Nations General Assembly and said: 'There must no longer be South Koreans and North Koreans, but just Koreans, who must be encouraged to work together to build their country with the advice and support of the United Nations.' This was an important change of policy as, instead of restoring the 'sovereignty' of South Korea, the aim was now to achieve the 'unity' of Korea. On 27 September, Washington, without waiting for any instruction from the United Nations, authorised MacArthur to cross the 38th Parallel. It was not until 6 October, in spite of a universal feeling of unease, the General Assembly voted its explicit approval to allow this to happen. Britain agreed to this extension of the war hoping that this would lead to a reunification of the whole of the Korean Peninsula and was still confident that China would not react to this by any military retaliation.

Macarthur's staff also continued to tell him that the Chinese would not invade and he believed them. The estimate of his Intelligence Staff was 'with our largely unopposed air forces with their atomic potential capable of destroying at will all bases of attack and lines of supply north as well as south of the Yalu; no Chinese military commander would dare hazard the commitment of large forces upon the Korean Peninsular. The risk of their utter destruction through lack of supply would be too great.' It is significant, however, that MacArthur also felt that if they were wrong and in the unlikely event the Chinese did invade and entered the war, then strategically it might be a good thing as it would be possible to employ his old tactic of a 'double prong' by using an intense bombing campaign against the Chinese infrastructure in the north, if necessary using atomic weapons, in conjunction with an invasion by Chiang Kai Shek from the south. He recognised that this might be a bloody affair, but was confident of success and felt that such a military operation would settle the Chinese Communist problem once and for all as it would restore a Government in Peking that was sympathetic to America and was the enemy of Moscow. This was the great difference between General MacArthur, and President Truman and the rest of the United Nations; MacArthur was not afraid of starting a Third World War. He had won battles in the First World War, defeated the might of Imperial Japan in the vast areas of the Pacific in the Second World War, successfully occupied and democratised Japan, and had defeated the North Korean Army by landing at Inchon. He was used to tackling big challenges and winning; he was not frightened by a war with China but saw it as the next step in the inevitable war against the evil spread of communism and was confident that the war could be won.

General Willoughby, his Senior Intelligence Advisor, supported him in this view and emphasised that the Chinese Communist Government had only been in power for a year and was still not in full control over their huge country. He described the Chinese Army as 'a combination of Asiatic cannon fodder and Soviet technical know-how, an army of illiterate Chinese coolies under the opiate of the Red gospel, reinforced with modern Russian tommy guns.' The Chinese have a saying: 'He who rides the tiger will find difficulty in getting off.' It was politicians who made the decision that military action was required to solve the situation in Korea; perhaps they did not remember that once military action begins, military commanders may have very different ideas about what constitutes victory. For

Macarthur the aim was to defeat the enemy and do this in the fastest way using every means possible that would reduce the number of his casualties. He knew that the Chinese and North Korean forces were being supplied with reinforcements, weapons, ammunition and logistical support from China and Russia; it was therefore a military imperative to stop this. He considered the best way to do this was by aerial bombardment. His orders were however clear: 'Under no circumstance will your forces cross the Manchurian or USSR borders of Korea and no Non-Korean ground forces will be used in the North East provinces bordering the Soviet Union or Manchurian borders. Furthermore, support of your operations north or south of the 38th Parallel will not include any air or naval action against Manchuria or against USSR territory.' The order is quite clear; MacArthur was not permitted to send Non-Korean ground forces up to the Yalu. This was the order he disobeyed and although Washington was aware of his disobedience they took no action. Dean Acheson is reported to have said: 'We sat around like rabbits while MacArthur carried out this nightmare.'

It now transpires that Moscow and Peking knew of this strict injunction to Macarthur limiting his actions only to North Korea with its implication that even if China did cross the border with a large army they would not suffer any retaliatory attack on their own country. The Western politicians' aim was to make sure everything was done to avoid a Third World War and they achieved this aim. The USSR was not faced by any act of aggression which forced it to retaliate and the Chinese, who felt it a necessity to support the North Koreans and remove the Americans from their border, were able to do so using the ludicrous but accepted euphemism that it was a People's Volunteer Army (PVA) which crossed into Korea not an Army of the Chinese State.

On 28 October 1950, after elements of the United Nations forces had reached the Yalu, an Intelligence Memorandum to the Joint Chiefs of Staff in Washington stated: 'Regular Chinese Forces in Manchuria now number 316,000 organised into 34 Divisions in 12 Corps. In addition there are 347,000 irregulars or Security Forces. All Regulars could be deployed in the Korean War. The bulk of these forces are now in position along the Yalu River and numerous crossing sites.

They assemble in complete safety since UN air forces are forbidden to cross the Border. Twenty-nine Divisions or two-thirds of the total known to be in Manchuria are immediately available.' Macarthur knew that his force was now outnumbered five-to-one and that each day this figure would grow worse. He had been told he could not go on the offensive and felt, therefore, he had been forced to adopt a defensive role where he had to maintain a line of defence with limited reserve capability and the Chinese could select their point of attack at the time that suited them. He objected strongly to this 'Maginot line of action' and began preparations for an offensive on the basis that if the Chinese did not intervene it would mean the end of the war and if they did intervene it would 'demolish the fiction of a Volunteer Army' and prove it was really the 'Regular Red Army' which gave him the right to strike enemy airbases in Communist China.

Such a policy was anathema to Washington and was exacerbated by the deep sense of animosity between President Truman and General MacArthur. The two men disliked each other intensely. MacArthur had been a Divisional Commander in the First World War, the youngest man to hold this appointment and had earned six silver stars. He had been the Commandant of West Point and had just won the War in the Pacific. In the First World War, Truman had been a captain in the Missouri National Guard and had no subsequent military experience. General MacArthur was occupying his position as a result of battle, and President Truman initially had his office because President Roosevelt had died. MacArthur distrusted politicians and Truman suspected that MacArthur had political aspirations. Since the Duke of Wellington the British have rejected the idea of a victorious military soldier becoming the country's political leader, and British generals shared this view. Famous as General Douglas Haig and General Bernard Montgomery became, neither would have contemplated trying to become Prime Minister. In the USA, however, it was different; there was a tradition of military leaders becoming political leaders, as in the case of President Eisenhower. Truman had reason to worry that MacArthur could become a rival for his office.

In 1945 Truman had gone out of his way to placate the autocracy of MacArthur, but had been rebuffed. The President had invited

MacArthur to return to America to be awarded the Distinguished Service Cross but he had declined. Truman sent personal representatives to Tokyo to discuss Far Eastern Policy. McArthur had kept them waiting and treated them with disdain. Truman had given explicit orders that MacArthur should not make public statements about Formosa in case this should lead China to think an invasion from the south was imminent, but MacArthur visited Formosa and in a draft speech to the Veterans of Foreign War which was leaked to the press, made the point: 'The military value of Taiwan should not be underestimated and that from Taiwan the United States can dominate with air power every Asiatic port from Vladivostok to Singapore and prevent any hostile movement into the Pacific.' This was in direct contradiction of Truman's policy and increased his anger. The question of crossing the Yalu was an issue which could have enormous international implications, and sadly this issue was significantly complicated by the fact that the Commander in Chief and his Commander on the ground disliked and distrusted each other.

By early October 1950, for Western politicians the situation was clear and looked good. As long as China did not interfere, they could continue with their policy of helping a united Korea develop into a democratic society free of the influence of Russia and China. They had stopped Macarthur taking military actions that he considered necessary to reduce communist influence in the Far East, and had made sure that both Russia and China knew that it was not their intention to cross the border and risk any chance of a Third World War. They knew that China had the capability to attack but they presumed that Peking was not going to risk attacking the United Nations in order to help Kim Il Sung retain control of the north. They were wrong. Mao Tse Tung had long been worried by the possibility of an attack by the USA. In March 1949, in a Conference Paper, he had written: 'When we make war plans, we have always to take into account the possibility that the US Government may send troops to occupy some of the coastal cities and fight us directly. We should continue to prepare for this now so as to avoid being taken by surprise.' He was reassured, however, that the United States did not intend to use the atom bomb in the Korean conflict as this fact had been stated publicly by Truman. This statement was particularly significant as the use of the atomic bomb is different from any other weapon held by the United States in that it is not in the possession or held on charge by the United States Military. Its use is 'only to the extent that the express consent and direction of the President of the United States has been obtained', and Truman at a Press Conference had stated he had no intention of using atomic weapons in Korea. In October 1950, when MacArthur had pushed his forces up to the borders of China along the Yalu River and was making bellicose noises about 'defeating the Red Menace', Mao decided that it was time to take the initiative and attack before being attacked. He had the superiority of numbers, the knowledge that the West did not want to extend the fighting into China, were against the use of the atomic bomb and, he thought, that if he invaded Korea now he would have a good chance of driving the United Nations out of Korea. He also initiated a propaganda masterstroke. The Chief of Staff in command of the Chinese forces, General Lin-Piao, was given approval to present his case to the United Nations Security Council, and here he took the opportunity to complain of 'American aggression against China'. It was a masterstroke. Kim Il Sung had distorted the fact of his invasion of the south by alleging the south had invaded the north, and now the Americans were accused of provoking China by their military actions across the Chinese border. Whereas in the West the military advances made by the North Koreans and the Chinese Volunteer Army in the first week of each invasion were clear proof of who perpetrated the aggression, there was a growing feeling of unease among the Third World Countries of American intentions in Korea and also about their growing interference in other sovereign nations. The accepted enemy of the USA was no longer Fascism or Japanese Imperialism, it was Communism and now this had been decided, it had become legitimate for the CIA to try to overthrow regimes that were sympathetic to Moscow. Third World Governments became aware that in the Middle East and in South America, CIA agents were funding dissident groups and providing arms to those who they considered would be more pro-American than pro-Russian. There was enough evidence to show that CIA agents had been operating in China and that American planes had violated Chinese airspace, and it was well known that Washington supported Chiang Kai Shek. Further, Macarthur's views on defeating China were public knowledge, so who was actually responsible for the fighting along the Yalu could be open to debate. It was always a matter of surprise to those fighting the war that what they considered to be a clear case of defending the south against armed aggression could be construed, not only by the Russian and Chinese people, but also by so many Third World countries to be part of a capitalist/imperialist plot.

CHAPTER SEVENTEEN

An Attack by Red China into North Korea is Not a Credible Proposition

The sad, almost unbelievable fact is that the assessment of the risk which was so wrong in June 1950 with regards to the North Korean invasion of the south was repeated in October 1950, with regard to the Chinese invasion. On 15 October 1950 at their meeting in Wake Island, Macarthur told Truman that there was little chance of a large-scale Chinese intervention and added that should it occur, his air power would destroy any Chinese forces that appeared. Next day the Chinese entered Korea. Two gross errors of judgement that resulted in the deaths of so many, including the soldiers of Baker Troop.

The ultimate responsibility for failing to recognise that the Red Army was going to cross the Yalu and enter the Korean War must fall on the shoulders of President Truman and even more so on General MacArthur. But these two men were 'operational' commanders and made executive decisions. It was the responsibility of the Intelligence Staff to provide them with the correct facts about the enemy's capabilities and intentions, and the Intelligence Staff, both military and civilian, got it wrong. The conclusion has to be that both Major General Charles Willoughby, the Far East Command Chief of Staff for Intelligence (G2) to MacArthur, and the Central Intelligence Agency responsible for advising the Joint Chiefs of Staff in Washington, accurately assessed the capability of the Red Army to attack, but erroneously assessed their intention to do so.

As regards their 'capability', by October 1950 the official figure of 450,000 Chinese troops available to launch an attack was correct, as were their estimates of the Chinese Order of Battle and dispositions along the Korean border. It was also correctly assessed that many of these divisions were experienced units that had combat experience both in the war against the Japanese and against the Nationalist Armies of General Chiang Kai Shek. They were known to have armoured units with T 34 tanks, heavy and medium artillery, and could move rapidly across bad terrain with little logistical support. As to the morale of the soldiers, it was also correctly assessed that this was high, and that although many soldiers were not necessarily committed communists, they believed that the Americans had taken the place of the Japanese who wished to occupy their country and they would fight determinedly to eject them but that, in comparison to the United Nations Air Force, the Chinese were numerically and technically very inferior, although this might alter if they received support from the Soviet Air Force.

As regards 'intention' there were many indicators. At 0300 hrs on 3 October, the Chinese Foreign Minister, Chou En Lai, summoned K.M. Pannikar the Indian Ambassador in Peking, and told him that 'if the US troops are going to cross the 38th Parallel in an attempt to extend the war and if the US troops really do so, we cannot sit idly by and remain indifferent. We will intervene.' This statement was also repeated publicly in Pyongyang in an expression of solidarity with the North Korean Government. Other indications of an impending attack included:

- The movement of large numbers of Chinese troops to the Border areas including two armies that had previously been stationed opposite Formosa.
- The appointment of General Peng Te Huai, a veteran of the Long March and the most famous and successful general in the war against the Nationalists, to be commander of the Chinese forces along the border.
- In the weeks leading up to the attack an increase in the hostile propaganda attacks charging the US with 'intervention and aggression' which in Taiwan, were assessed as 'may be

providing an excuse for Chinese Communist interventions.'
• The improvement in facilities to support its air force in close proximity to the Sino-Korean Border.
• The strengthening of the Manchurian Border defences.
• Reports from Nationalist sources in Taiwan that 'the Communists on the Mainland intend to intervene in Korea.'
• Reports from agents run by US Special Forces who had been recruited and then sent back to join the Red Army that preparations were being made to invade North Korea.

However, in spite of all these indications, in Washington the Secretary of State Dean Acheson reflected the opinion of the 'China experts' and the CIA who felt that the Communist Government had not recovered from its long civil war and would not have the intention to start a war because:

• It did not have the required number of trained troops.
• It feared its internal control of the country would be weakened.
• There was little advantage to China following from such a war.
• The probability of China's international position would be weakened and it might be detrimental to their application for a seat in the United Nations.

General Willoughby also felt that if China had the intention to go to war it would have attacked when the United Nations were most vulnerable:

• When it had surrounded the weak garrison in the Pusan Perimeter.
• Or, just after the Inchon landings before the United Force had joined with the break-out force from Pusan.
• Or, before a stronger force supported by a strong air force had reached the Yalu.

Thus, the CIA, the Joint Chiefs of Staff and General Willoughby remained completely confident that the Chinese would not attack. Willoughby was especially certain because, as he said, he could not believe that an 'illiterate Asian Peasant Army would be stupid enough to attack the might of America and its Allies.' Such was the confidence that MacArthur had in the assessments of Willoughby that by September 1950 he was confidently predicting victory in North Korea, agreed that two divisions could return from the Far East to Europe – one of whom he selected to be the 2nd (Indian Head) Division which had fought so well in the Pusan Perimeter – and made no objection to the decision to divert ammunition ships away from the Far East. 'Home for Christmas' was the cry.

In the advance up to the Yalu, MacArthur had divided his force into two wings; on the west, a direct movement forward by the Eighth Army towards the enemy capital of Pyongyang, and on the east, an amphibious movement by Ten Corps commanded by General Almond to the east coast port of Wonsan to bring flank pressure if necessary for the capture of Pyongyang. In the period of the advance MacArthur would control and coordinate both wings until they met in the north when General Walker would resume united command. The reason for this division of command was the impossibility for Walker in the west to attempt the command responsibility, the coordination, and especially the logistic resupply lines of the east coastal area. On the west coast, resupply had to be done through Inchon, the port whose adverse tidal conditions had aroused such violent opposition to the concept of the amphibious landing, and on the east coast there was the need to establish a new and independent seaborne supply line direct from Japan to Wosan.

In the event, the march north went far quicker than anyone expected. The challenge was who would reach Pyongyang first and it was the ROK Division that won. The enemy faded away. On 27 September there was still no belief that the Chinese would attack, and the order from the Joint Chiefs of Staff to MacArthur remained: 'You will continue to make special efforts to determine whether there is a Chinese Communist or Soviet threat to the attainment of your objective.' The advance continued peacefully towards the Chinese border until gradually the unbelievable news became known that under cover of darkness a Chinese People's Volunteer Army of thirty-eight divisions, 300,000 men in fighting formations, had begun to cross over the Yalu to face four US and four ROK divisions. The Communists had launched Phase One of their invasion. The orders from Mao Tse Tung to General Peng Te Huai were to hold the United Nations Advanced Guard, then march behind the main body of the Eighth Army and Ten Corps to cut their lines of communication, then to 'run them all the way back to Pyongyang and if they retreat, strike down to the 38th Parallel.'

The attack started, and was reported by General Walker at the time: 'An ambush and surprise attack has begun a sequence of events leading to the complete collapse and disintegration of the Second South Korean Corps of three Divisions. The Corps retreated in confusion to a position thirteen miles from the only crossing area into the 1st US Corps combat zone before some semblance of order could be restored.' In Washington and in Macarthur's headquarters there was still a conviction that the invasion force was not Chinese but was North Korean, and in spite of intense aerial reconnaissance certainly no trace of any huge movement by the Chinese forces could be seen. As a flow of interrogation reports began to arrive providing evidence of Chinese involvement, they were discounted on the grounds that the prisoners were North Koreans who were residents in China and who had volunteered to fight. So firmly was the belief that the Chinese would not attack that there was a desperate attempt made to find evidence that it was not happening. General Paik Sun Yup, a divisional commander in the Korean Army was sent to interview a prisoner and confirm his nationality, but was alarmed and depressed to discover that the prisoner made no secret of the fact he was Chinese, had been in the Nationalist Army and was now part of a huge force currently crossing into Korea. The CIA also began to recognise the new situation, and after reports from the US Embassy in The Hague arrived that Chinese troops had moved into Korea, it began to change its firm view that there would be no invasion. It abandoned the position that the Chinese had the capability to intervene but would not do so, and began to accept that the Chinese had entered Korea although it still held the view that China had no intention of entering the war in any large scale.

It was not until 2 November that MacArthur reported to

Washington that 'recent captures of soldiers of Chinese nationality and information obtained from their interrogators, together with increased resistance being encountered by advancing UN forces, removes the problem of Chinese intervention from the realms of the academic and turns it into a serious proximate threat.' The following day he sent a revised Communist Order of Battle listing in numerical detail the strength and location in Manchuria of fifty-six regular army divisions in sixteen corps which, together with district security forces made a total of 868,000 men with more converging from Central China. In spite of this huge increase in the numbers of his enemy, MacArthur was told that he could expect no major addition to his own forces and his request for Nationalist troops from Formosa was denied. He was told that this action would 'disrupt the united position of the nations associated with the United States in the United Nations and leave the United States isolated. The utmost care will be necessary to avoid the disruption of the essential Allied Line up in that organisation.' Up to now, the United Nations had been a compliant partner in the war and how it had developed. This was the first time that the United States recognised that the advantages of sailing under the United Nations banner could also bring its drawbacks. No one in the United Nations wanted to risk an extension of the war by bringing Chiang Kai Shek into the battle and the General Assembly refused to consider sending extra troops.

MacArthur now had to consider what to do. He decided that to pull back Ten Corps to Wonsan and form a defensive line with the Eighth Army would be fatal, as each division would have a front of over twenty miles with no reserve force to create a defence in depth. He also recognised that given the tactics of infiltration so frequently and efficiently employed by the Chinese, they could easily subject his entire line to piecemeal destruction. He decided, therefore, to adopt the old Napoleonic adage 'When all seems lost –Attack' and so he rejected a 'Maginot Line Plan of Action', consulted his staff and field commanders and ordered that a 'limited advance that kept the Army free to manoeuvre was the best solution to an extraordinary situation.'

He did, however, order Walker to prepare, and have ready for instant use, a plan 'for immediate retreat if the Chinese should intervene.' The Eighth Army began its cautious move forward but on 26 November the Chinese committed themselves to total involvement and launching Phase Two of their invasion, and went into battle against the United States, albeit fighting as the United Nations. The Chinese Fourth Army ferociously attacked the Eighth Army under Walker and the Third Chinese Army attacked Ten Corps under General Almond. MacArthur, very bitter about the lack of support and intelligence he had received, now decided that withdrawal was the right answer. He would fight delaying actions long enough for Almond to evacuate by sea from Wonsan and then join Walker to form a new defensive line farther south. His plan was to form a new defensive line and then resume the offensive, counting on forcing the Chinese supply lines out of the 'sanctuary area' where he could hit them with incessant air attacks. So began the great 'Bug Out'. On 21 November Walker reported that elements of Ten Corps and reconnaissance elements of the Eighth Army had reached the Yalu River, but then gave the abrupt and surprising order, 'Stop. Go back!' It was at this time that the Chinese representative, who had been allowed to speak in the United Nations in a brilliant propaganda coup which convinced so many countries who were against the war, emotionally announced that the American forces had invaded China. They had not, but they had reached the Chinese border and it was alleged that certain American commanders had joyfully relieved themselves into the waters of the Yalu River.

To add to Macarthur's anger, as soon as it was known that the Chinese were crossing the Yalu, he requested that the six bridges they were using should be destroyed by the Air Force. Washington denied this request, as Willoughby subsequently wrote: 'These bridges still stand. Their planks have echoed to the tramping of hundreds of thousands of men, and millions of tons of supplies and ammunition have crossed them, either to support the enemy or blast our own ranks. They are still there inviolate.' His view was that the forbidding of the all-out bombardment of the bridges meant that half a dozen American divisions were exposed to the full onslaught of overwhelming numbers. He felt the Chinese were not only assured that the United Nations had no real intention of winning, but China would be therefore guaranteed against the risk of losing. Macarthur has described the withdrawal as made with consummate skill and one of the best operations – if not the best – he had ever made and that the hard decisions he made and the skill displayed by his field commanders in their implementation of the withdrawal 'had saved not only the Eighth Army but also Korea itself and with it our future hopes for the Far East.' He was right in that the withdrawal did preserve the United Nations Army, but I suspect that to the gunners of Baker Troop the whole affair does seem to have been what they would describe as a pretty big screw up.

CHAPTER EIGHTEEN

The Great Retreat

For the soldiers who fought in Korea, now began the most dangerous and difficult period of the war. The weather was frighteningly cold, the roads to the south overcrowded and deteriorating, and the Chinese tactics were to march through the mountains by night to avoid being bombed and then set ambushes along routes which the wheeled and tracked vehicles had to follow. An air of 'Sauve Qui Peut' spread quickly, especially amongst the logistic and non-combat units. British troops have vivid memories of truck drivers, cigars glowing in their mouths, speeding past the marching infantry columns. As one truck dashed past the driver leant out and yelled: 'You had better hurry. The Gooks are right behind' to which a tired British soldier, who perhaps had memories of Dunkirk, Calais, Tobruk or Singapore responded: 'No hurry. We've done this before.' To the cry 'Why are you bugging out', came the reply 'We ain't bugging out. We are retreating.' and they were right. MacArthur and all his senior generals had come to the conclusion that to save the United Nations force it was imperative to pull back to another line where they could establish coordinated defensive positions that would extend the Chinese lines of communication, which could then be destroyed by air and sea bombardments, and give time for a new advance to be organised. As Willoughby pointed out: 'Land does not matter in a war, it is the final victory that counts.' It was a strategy used in many past military campaigns well known as 'Recule pour mieux sauté.' For the public it was, however, a devastating reversal, especially when pictures were flashed around the world of retreating American troops in the most pitiable of weather conditions. It was made worse because only weeks before, the message had been one of 'the boys are coming home and we will be celebrating a joyful victorious Christmas.'

Two typical articles in the American press were:

> The flight of our troops before Chinese peasant soldiers was the most shameful disgrace suffered by American arms since the First Battle of Bull Run in 1861.

> It was America's worst licking since the Battle of the Bulge and maybe even Pearl Harbor. Barring a military miracle, the Army might have to be evacuated in a new Dunkirk from being lost in a new Bataan.

Willoughby pointed out that after the entry of China into the war, the American Army was compelled to take odds never before encountered in the entire military history of the Nation: 'It is impossible to understand on a professional basis how the General Staff in Washington could placidly accept the staggering odds piled on the Eighth Army in Korea. Instead of a pat on the back for our teenage draftees of a few months training who were fighting rather forlornly in an alien land, we were engulfed in an inexplicable wave of defeatist reports. Once again it was the soldiers on the ground that paid the price of strategic mistakes.'

The feeling of gloom spread to the CIA, which in their National Intelligence Estimate 'Probable Soviet Moves to Exploit the Present Situation' published in December 1950 concluded that 'the Soviets would assess their current military and political position as one of great strength in comparison with that of the west, and that they will propose to exploit the apparent conviction of the west of its own present weakness.' At that time there was no assumption that China and the Soviet Union would differ on policy and they assessed that the joint Moscow/Peking aims for 1951 would be:

- 1. Withdrawal of UN Forces from Korea and of the Seventh Fleet from Formosan waters.
- 2. Establishment of Communist China as the predominant power in the Far East including the seating of Communist China in the United Nations.
- 3. Reduction of Western control over Japan as a step toward its eventual elimination.

- 4. Prevention of West German rearmament.
- 5. 'It can be anticipated that irrespective of any moves looking toward negotiations, assuming virtual Western surrender is not involved, the Kremlin plans a continuation of Chinese Communist pressure in Korea until the military defeat of the UN is complete.'

These were a very optimistic set of aims for the Chinese and North Korean Armies to achieve, but given the disaster that had happened to the UN Forces in November and December 1950, they could have been seen to be achievable. For the troops north of the 38th Parallel it was a disastrous, painful and frightening experience. At the Chosin Reservoir, the 1st US Marine Division, including the British 41 Commando, was completely surrounded and in terrible winter conditions with the temperature dropping to minus forty degrees, had managed to fight its way out covered by maritime air support. It had been confronted by four Chinese Divisions and its successful withdrawal to the Port at Hungnam was a unique example of a division retaining its command capability, cohesion and fighting spirit in the sad saga of the mass retreat following the Chinese invasion. On 24 December Ten Corps evacuated the last of its troops from north-east Korea.

For the troops of the Eighth Army it meant moving south back down the road that the Engineers had tried to improve some weeks before. The road wound its way through mountain ranges and was dominated on both sides. The critical stretch of this 'gauntlet' was about five miles south of Kunuri and was known as 'The Pass' where the Chinese laid their ambushes. The first to move through 'The Pass' were the heavy equipment vehicles of the Engineers, but they were soon hit and set on fire. The main column which followed was led by tanks of the US 2nd Division but they were also stopped when they ran into the debris of the Engineers and the burnt-out vehicles of the Turkish Brigade which had tried to break through in a relief attempt and had been caught in crossfire. The troops following behind the tanks were now subjected to continuous machine gun, rifle and mortar fire. Many tried to hide in ditches along the road and were killed; others waited until night and in scattered groups tried to make their way back. One of the worst days in the history of the American army was on 30 November 1950 when in the 2nd US Division the 9th Regiment lost an estimated 1,474 men; the 38th Regiment 1,178 and the 23rd Regiment 545. The retreat continued and covered over 120 miles in ten days. Huge bonfires lit the whole area where attempts were made to burn vast quantities of stores and ammunition. In Pyongyang, piles of equipment and clothing had been stacked and this gave the opportunity for British troops to exchange summer clothing for cold weather clothing. It was then that Brigadier Coad gave the very sensible order that the British troops could take and wear whatever was warm but that they must wear their own regimental headdress. Rations and weapons taken from the stores left behind in Pyongyang could be found in British regiments for months to follow, but large quantities fell into the hands of the pursuing Chinese. Figures published later revealed that although in the whole of the Second World War the US Army only lost 53 guns from being overrun or having surrendered, from July 1950 until December 1950 the Eighth Army lost 142 artillery pieces to the enemy.

On 23 December General Walker, commanding the Eighth Army, was killed in a traffic accident. A truck had pulled out in front of his speeding jeep which flipped over and he died instantly. Washington chose General Mathew Bunker Ridgeway to fly out and take his place and he arrived three days later on 26 December. It proved to be a turning point in the war. Ridgeway had commanded the Airborne Forces, which had landed on D Day, 6 June 1944, and by 1 December 1951 was acknowledged to be one of the 'best fighting Generals in the US Army'. When he arrived, the Eighth Army had retreated over 300 miles since 30 November and was occupying a line below the 38th Parallel but which included the Capital City of Seoul. On New Year's Eve, the Chinese began the third phase of their plan which successfully broke the United Nations forces in the east, centre and the west that included 29 Commonwealth Brigade. Seoul was evacuated and the Chinese advanced to the north bank of the Han River. Mao Tse Tung was convinced that victory was possible and Peking Radio was confidently predicting that the Americans were going to be 'run into the sea.' Ridgeway decided to establish a new line of defence called 'Line D' and made his first request to

Washington for additional troops – ten more National Guard artillery units.

It is very interesting that as late as April 1951, although there were still strict orders in place that UN pilots could not fly in 'hot pursuit' over the Yalu, Ridgeway was very worried that the Chinese Air Force might enter the war in support of their 'Volunteer Army' by launching massive air strikes from Manchuria and the Chinese Shantung Peninsula. He requested authority from the US Joint Chiefs of Staff for reconnaissance flights over these areas and also discussed requesting authority for a pre-emptive strike on airfields prior to an offensive from Manchuria. On 27 April Ridgeway sent a top secret message to the joint chiefs:

> 'I have concluded that the military situation in the theatre now requires that there should be delegated to me without delay the authority to attack airbases in Manchuria and the Shantung Peninsular at the earliest moment. I am prepared to do this following a major enemy attack against our forces in Korea and I would define a major air attack as a concerted effort by a large number of enemy combat aircraft against our ground forces, rear bases or fleet and not merely counter-air action such as recent enemy MIG operations.

On 28 April the joint chiefs told Ridgeway: 'You are authorised to use the United States Air Force to conduct air reconnaissance of the enemy air bases in Manchuria and the Shantung Peninsular, such reconnaissance should if practicable be made at high altitude and as surreptitiously as possible.' The Joint Chiefs then advised that if the Communists launched a major air attack against United Nations Forces in Korea, Ridgeway was authorised to carry out offensive operations. This significant decision that the USA was prepared to bomb China was not discussed with their Allies and had been taken some weeks earlier by the Joint Chiefs of Staff, the Secretary of Defense George C. Marshall and Truman. However, they had decided not to tell MacArthur as they feared he might use this authority to justify 'premature action and enlarge the war.' It was part of the deep suspicion held in Washington that MacArthur could no longer be trusted to carry out the orders of Truman, his Commander in Chief and that the war should be limited to a 'police action'. It was the firm view that whatever the tactical cost of allowing China and Russia the great advantage of 'safe havens', this cost had to be borne in order to reduce the risk of a Third World War.

MacArthur was still convinced, however, that China had to be defeated and that the way to do this was by using the atomic bomb and allowing the Nationalist Army to invade from Taiwan. Truman was totally against this policy and decided MacArthur had to be relieved of his command. He asked the Joint Chiefs of Staff for their views. It was a very, very difficult decision for them. It meant sacking a senior officer in the middle of a war in which only weeks before they had been praising him for the brilliant operation at Inchon and was an officer who had won the Presidential Medal of Honor, was the acknowledged victor of the War in the Pacific, the commander who had successfully brought democracy to Japan, who had kept his promise 'I will return' after being thrown out of the Philippines, and who was a hugely popular hero in America. But the Joint Chiefs of Staff agreed he had to go. It would be wrong to blame personal animosity on the part of Truman for the division in policy concerning the possibility of launching a war against China. On 15 May 1950, General Omar Bradley, chairman of the Joint Chiefs of Staff, agreed with Truman and stated: 'Red China is not a powerful nation seeking to dominate the world. Frankly in the opinion of the Joint Chiefs of Staff this strategy would involve us in the wrong war, at the wrong time and with the wrong enemy.'

They therefore supported the dismissal of MacArthur.

The solution was a remarkable paradox. MacArthur was abruptly sacked but then granted a hero's return, given more honours, and allowed a hugely successful ticker-tape parade through New York followed by the privilege of talking to a joint session on Capital Hill. His removal was universally accepted as the right decision. The way he was treated by Truman on his return was universally regarded as brilliant.

.

Part Three

Lessons from the War in Korea

* * *

CHAPTER NINETEEN

Manipulation of Intelligence

The influence of General Charles Willoughby on the Korean Campaign is extremely significant and is very similar to the influence of General John Charteris, Senior Intelligence Officer to General Haig in the First World War. Both men served closely with their commanders for a long time, shared bitter defeats, successful campaigns and a great distrust, almost hatred, of senior headquarters and politicians. Both felt that military intelligence about the enemy helped make military operational decisions, but that politicians used military intelligence for their own status and diplomatic influence. Charteris and Willoughby were not only the providers of intelligence but were also close friends of their commanders. Each became emotionally entwined with their commander's feelings and intentions, and found it more and more tempting and comforting to provide intelligence that matched their commander's operational plans rather than be bearers of bad news. From scratch in 1914, General Charteris developed a most successful intelligence acquisition infrastructure, combining signals intelligence, photographic intelligences, and interrogation intelligence, intelligence from forward combat units plus terrain and climatic intelligence. The flow of intelligence was rapid and was analysed by specialists at every level of command. It was a remarkable achievement and, by 1917, was producing accurate estimates of the German Order of Battle, dispositions, artillery and armour. Willoughby had done the same in the Pacific War and had provided MacArthur with a first-class intelligence service. The similarity between Charteris and Willoughby is that both men conformed to the ancient adage that 'if you control the intelligence, you control the decision making.' They ensured, therefore, that they were the focal point of all intelligence being briefed to their general, and both men were bitterly resentful and hostile to any intelligence agency that suggested a different view of the enemy to the one they were giving their commander. If there were dissenting indications that did not conform to their own briefing, they would add a comment negating the reliability of the source.

For Willoughby the CIA was suspect, politically motivated, and lacked the reality of those serving on the ground. This was exactly the same view that Charteris held of the Intelligence Department in the War Office in London. When Charteris was sick and was temporarily replaced by another officer, the replacement was amazed and very disconcerted by the difference in the reports given by Charteris to his commander and the more sober reports and assessments being produced from London.

The responsibility on the shoulders of a senior commander in war grows as the operational situation develops. It is inevitable and understandable, therefore, that he will create a nucleus of staff officers around him who are not only competent, but also loyal to him and like him. They become his 'team', support his views, share his dislikes and they protect him from his enemies. General Eisenhower took his selected close operational and intelligence staff with him throughout the European Campaign; General Montgomery took his staff with him when he was posted back to Europe from Italy, MacArthur, whose strong personality and self confident arrogance especially needed a protective circle of staff officers around him, selected his close staff with great care. They gave him loyalty and affection and he returned the same.

To be a member of this close 'family' was a privilege and the qualification for admittance was proof of competence and the ability to get things done. If there was a problem that had to be raised it had to be accompanied by a solution. If it was an operational issue the operational commander had to respond with a positive and achievable response. The same went if it was an engineer problem of building bridges, road construction, building airfields or laying minefields. The response had to be 'can do'. Similarly, the huge logistical problems of land and sea transportation, of food and ammunition supply, equipment repair or medical support were all challenges that could be expressed, but then had to be followed by a solution. For the Intelligence Officer, his position in this close family is different; he can give a wonderful analysis of the enemy's capabilities and intentions, but it is not his responsibility to suggest measures to counter the potential dangers he is explaining. To do so leads to a lack of objectivity and distortion of the intelligence. Continual repetition of the enemy's potential can appear a misunderstanding of the commander's problems and even disloyal. There is, therefore, always strong pressure to be optimistic – which sadly can lead to fatal mistakes. Charteris said that if he kept reporting bad news, General Haig would be depressed all day and it was not his role to encourage this depression. No intelligence officer wants to gain the reputation of continually reporting possible disasters so that he can subsequently say, 'I told you so.' Too much negative reporting inevitably means he will lose the confidence of his commander who sees him not as someone who is seeking to help him solve problems but is someone who continually adds to his problems. Charteris not only briefed optimistically but on one occasion, in order to confirm his briefing on the poor state of the German Army, took Haig to see German prisoners of war, having first ordered that all the fit-looking prisoners should be removed from the cage. Willoughby knew that MacArthur did not believe the North Koreans would attack in June 1950 and that the Chinese would not attack in November 1950. He therefore briefed in line with this belief. The hardest task for an Intelligence Officer is to tell the commander what he does not want to hear and both Charteris and Willoughby failed to do this. A classic example of what happens when you do tell your commander the unpalatable truth was in September 1944 before the Battle of Arnhem. The Parachute Division had been preparing for this drop over several months; three times it had been told it was to happen and three times told to stand down. It was an intensely frustrating time for General 'Boy' Browning, the commander of such a well-trained and aggressively-minded corps, and he was determined not to be thwarted again. At the critical moment intelligence reports from Dutch Resistance fighters and from ULTRA, the top-secret capability for decoding intercepted radio traffic, warned of tanks arriving in the vicinity of the bridge at Arnhem. These disturbing reports reached Major Brian Urquhart, the senior Intelligence Officer reporting to Browning and he decided to request air reconnaissance to be flown over the Arnhem area. Eight sorties were flown on 12 and 16 September and among the photos taken were five oblique-angle pictures which showed the 'unmistakable presence of German armour'. Urquhart took these pictures to Browning, who could not countenance another delay to his operation so rejected the evidence and sent Urquhart to his Chief Medical Officer, suggesting he was mentally unbalanced and should be 'treated as a nervous child suffering from a nightmare and sent home on sick leave.' The Medical Officer's diagnosis was that Urquhart was 'suffering from nervous strain and exhaustion' and he was sent home. Urquhart was dismayed at the rejection of his intelligence, but felt more devastated that he was refused permission to drop with his colleagues. The Panzer tanks were there and were a major factor in the destruction of the Parachute Division in what became know as the battle of 'A Bridge too Far'.

Charteris distorted his final assessment about the German intention to attack in 1917 and Haig believed him with disastrous results for the British and French Armies. Willoughby distorted his final assessment about the North Korean intention to attack in June 1950 and the Chinese decision to invade in November 1950 with disastrous results for the United Nations and, in particular, the US forces. After their failures both officers were subjected to a deluge of unconstrained attacks on their professional capabilities and Charteris was sacked. For Willoughby the attacks centred around three issues; first that he did not warn his general of the impending invasion by North Korea, second that he did not warn his general of the consequences of crossing the 38th Parallel, and thirdly that he did not warn him that the Red Army was going to cross the Yalu and start a war with the United Nations which meant in reality starting a war with the United States. Perhaps understandably, the criticisms do not take into account his correct predictions throughout the Pacific War where he was constantly right and continually earned the praise and respect of his general for being right. For the three issues raised in the Korean War, Willoughby made a robust defence; first that North Korea was not the responsibility of his commander and therefore it was not his role to cross command boundaries and institute intelligence acquisition projects or to make assessments which were laid down as the responsibility of Washington secondly, on the issue of crossing the 38th Parallel, he had warned his general of the possible consequences but Truman and a United Nations Resolution had given approval for this crossing to take place; and lastly, as to the invasion by China into Korea, he had presented a very accurate picture of the 'capability' of the Chinese Army, including their dispositions and command structure. What he could not know was the intention of the Chinese to launch an attack and this required intelligence coming from inside China and especially from Peking. This was the responsibility of the diplomats and covert intelligence agencies who had failed to supply this vital intelligence.

There was also subsequent criticism that he had not listened to a myriad of facts that ran counter to his final assessment and only passed on to his general a picture that conformed to his general's operational plans. It may be that his final assessments were moulded to suit his general's wishes, but the comment that he discarded other allegedly more accurate reports from a number of junior officers is what he was paid to do. His briefings to MacArthur had to be the distillation of all the intelligence he had received and then to make a clear statement of what it meant. There are always junior intelligence staff officers who, after a failure, are happy to remember their own correct advice.

The criticism which is harder to discount is that although North Korea was not on his general's 'patch', an invasion by the North into South Korea would inevitably involve and affect his commander, and he should have taken a greater personal interest in this potential danger. As to the invasion by the Red Army crossing the Yalu, given his knowledge of the 'capability', regardless of Macarthur's deeply held, almost fanatical belief that this was not a credible proposition, he should have continually, determinedly, bluntly and with growing anger insisted that the 'capability' danger required an operational response. This was his failure; he manipulated the intelligence to suit his commander's wishes. It is a lesson that is as relevant today as it was in the Korean War.

CHAPTER TWENTY

Prisoners and Propaganda

The lessons learned from the way the Chinese treated our prisoners during the Korean War resulted in a significant change in the training we gave to prepare our military forces for conduct after capture, and subsequently led us to considerable difficulties in Northern Ireland. In the Second World War the rules of conduct after capture were simple, straightforward and easily understood. As a prisoner you gave only four facts:

- 1: Number
- 2: Rank
- 3: Name
- 4: Date of Birth

With servicemen, apart from aircrew, the Germans were mainly concerned with tactical information which would help them complete their Order of Battle of British Forces and, with luck, give an indication of possible offensives. For aircrew there was great interest in our navigational and bombing techniques and technical capability, but the time that could be allotted to any prisoner was limited and in a relatively short space of time the prisoner would find himself in a Stalag with his compatriots. Prisoners in the Korean War faced a totally different scenario. The Chinese, not the North Koreans, wanted to convert the prisoners to a belief in communism and, as a side effect, use them for propaganda purposes. The intense pressure put on the prisoners, which was a combination of rewards and punishment, did succeed in dividing the prisoners between the 'progressives' who went along with the propaganda, and the 'reactionaries' who were aggressively against the propaganda. The majority of the prisoners, however, took the easy and perhaps sensible option of not blatantly falling into either camp. Those who did and became 'progressives', although very small in number, were used most effectively by the Chinese in the diplomatic war that was being fought at the Peace Talks in Panmunjom. The first talks had begun in July 1951 and continued spasmodically until 27 July 1953 when the agreement was signed. Apart from the machinations of President Syngman Rhee, who bitterly opposed any agreement which would perpetuate the division of his country, the main dispute was the manner in which the prisoners would be released. It was a matter of face. During the war the United Nations had captured 130,000 North Koreans and 20,000 Chinese and imprisoned over 218,000 civilians all of whom had been put into camps on the Island of Koje-Do. Initially it seemed the easy solution would be to allow the total release of all prisoners back to their own countries. The problem arose in that thousands of Korean prisoners did not want to go back to the north, and many of the Chinese, who had served in the Army of Chiang Kai Shek and had been forcibly recruited into the Red Army, did not want to go back to China but wanted to go to Taiwan. The United States had announced that, as a matter of principle, they would not force any prisoner who did not wish to go back to North Korea or China to do so, and the British supported this view. At the end of the Second World War when Russia demanded that all Russian prisoners of war must be returned, there had been desperate and heartrending scenes when British officers had to deceive Russian prisoners who did not wish to return to Russia by telling them they were going to camps in West Germany, but then putting them into covered trucks and driving them into East Germany. The Russian prisoners knew that if they were sent back to Russia, they would be shot or sent to Siberia, and they were. There were senior British Army officers, particularly those in the Guards Armoured Brigade, who had to carry out this deception and who felt it was the most distressing episode in the whole war, even more distressing than seeing the sights of the concentration camps. This then was the dilemma – whether the United Nations continued fighting and suffering casualties or sent prisoners back against their will. Some meetings lasted several days, other times there was a gap of weeks with both sides unwilling to compromise. The breakthrough came in March 1953 when Stalin died and Malenkov, the new Premier, proposed a resumption of the talks and announced that the Communists would agree to an immediate exchange of sick and wounded prisoners. This operation was called 'Little Switch' and more than 600 United Nations soldiers were released in exchange for more than 6,000 North Korean and Chinese. Some of the United Nations soldiers released were found not to be sick or wounded and there was a suspicion that they included a number of 'progressives' who would speak well of their time in captivity. Little Switch was a start, but the issue of forced repatriation had not been resolved.

The situation on Koje-Do Island was proving very difficult; the camp was split into compounds, and in order to avoid bloodshed it was easier to put those who wished to return home to North Korea and China in their compounds, and those who wished to remain in separate compounds. Within the compounds and in line with the Geneva Convention, prisoners could elect their own representatives and these elected leaders imposed strict and ruthless discipline; murders of those opposing the leadership were commonplace. One leader of the Communist compound was a senior Communist cadre who had arranged to be captured so he could take control in the camp. The elected leaders in the non-Communist compounds were ex-Chiang Kai Shek senior officers who were equally ruthless. American control was minimal and the guard force was predominantly ROK soldiers. Following a series of riots, in an attempt to regain control American troops entered the camp and in the ensuing fighting seventy-seven prisoners were killed and two hundred injured. General Dodd, commanding Koje-Do, decided to mediate and went to the gates to talk to the leaders, but a party of prisoners who had been working outside the camp returned, seized him and forced him into the compound where he was held hostage. General Colson was sent to replace him and in order to obtain Dodd's release, signed a document stating: 'I can assure you that in the future, prisoners of war can expect humane treatment. I will do all in my power to eliminate future violence and bloodshed.' This apparent apology was seized upon by Peking and Moscow and was widely distributed as proof of American cruelty to their prisoners, together with pictures alleging, 'unarmed prisoners being shot.'

Colson and Dodd were officially reprimanded and reduced to the rank of colonel. It was a propaganda coup against the Americans and in order to dilute international adverse publicity, on 19 May 1952 General Mark Clark, who had taken over as Supreme Commander from MacArthur, suggested that a review should be carried out on the feasibility of 'internationalising' the guard duties. He felt that having forces from other UN countries share the responsibility had 'definite political advantages'. As a result, orders were given for a battalion from the Netherlands, a company from the Greek contingent, a company from the Royal Canadian Regiment and a company from the KSLI to be sent to the island. The British Government was upset that the British troops had been sent on this prison-guarding task without its knowledge and there were fierce debates in the House of Commons as to whether the British troop guarding the prisoners should be allowed to open fire. The Canadian Government was also very upset that its troops had been sent without the permission of Ottawa, and the Canadian Ambassador in Washington urged the State Department to rescind or suspend the deployment of the Canadian troops. However, the Commonwealth troops did go, but thereafter no Commonwealth troops were dispatched on tasks without the agreement of the General Officer Commanding the Commonwealth division.

In Panmunjom the talks continued, although there was great unease in the Commonwealth that the Americans would not allow a Commonwealth representative to be on the negotiation team. The issue at the time was how to confirm the fact that people who refused to go home were doing so voluntarily. It was decided therefore that a 'screening' process should be arranged, whereby a representative of the country concerned would interview the prisoners and try to persuade them to return home. To the fury of the Communists, after this had taken place, out of over 300,000 prisoners only 70,000 wished to be repatriated, which led them to allege that the screening process was a charade and prisoners were being pressurised and blackmailed not to return. Radios had been smuggled into the Communist compounds from China and orders were given that a breakout should take place that could be of great propaganda value to the Communists. To thwart this uprising, on 10 June American Airborne troops entered the Communist compound and armed with tear gas, concussion grenades, bayonets, pick helves, flame-throwers and tanks, took control. Thirty-three prisoners were killed and 139 were wounded. One American soldier was speared to death. This use of violence was what the Chinese had hoped for and they launched a worldwide publicity campaign with pictures of alleged American brutality alongside pictures of United Nations prisoners playing sport, holding theatrical shows, smiling and looking happy. It was a precedent for using prisoners in military custody for propaganda purposes that was to be repeated in Northern Ireland twenty years later. In spite of these difficulties over the return of prisoners there was a positive wish by both sides to reach an agreement, and the talks continued even though Rhee, when he learned that agreement might be reached without the unification of Korea, on his own initiative arranged for the release of 24,000 of the 35,000 North Koreans who had refused repatriation. The system agreed was that those who did not wish to return home would be detained for a further ninety days after the ceasefire under the protection of Indian guards. Those countries concerned could then appoint 'examiners' who would be allowed to talk to each prisoner in turn and try to persuade him to come home. It was not a success. When the examiners visited the Communist compounds the prisoners, under the direction of their 'elected' leaders, shouted and banged containers and refused to allow them to meet with any individual on their own. The result was that very few of the 23,000 Chinese prisoners and 325 Koreans who had initially stated they did not wish to return home agreed to change their mind. The same thing happened in the prison camp in North Korea where twenty-one American soldiers and one British Royal Marine were being held who also had refused to return home. They too, banged on containers and refused to allow the examiner to meet any individual on his own.

The fact that these United Nations soldiers had freely decided to go to China rather than return home was a great advantage to the Communists in countering the fact that hundreds of others did not wish to do so, and in the UK a detailed research programme was started as to why they had made this decision. An analysis of these twenty-one Americans showed that all had been captured in the desperate fighting in October and November 1950 when the United Nations had been driven back from the Yalu in the middle of a Korean winter, that all but one had been in the Army for less than a year before capture, and that all had been designated 'progressives' before the ceasefire was signed. There was no common denominator of social background or religion, and the effort the Communists had put into recruiting African-American soldiers had failed as only one decided to stay. The conclusion was that very early after capture these men had opted to acquiesce to the propaganda in order to gain better living conditions and were then gradually sucked into a position where it was easier to continue to conform and co-operate rather than disagree.

The decision of the twenty-two to stay in China was a success for the Chinese at the time, even though the Communist beliefs they had adopted did not last very long. In the end, all but one of the twenty-two returned home. Corporal Adams, the only African-American, married a Chinese girl but returned to America in 1966 and opened a Chinese restaurant in Memphis. The remainder either attended universities or worked in collective farms or factories in China before returning home. One married a Polish girl and went to live in Poland but returned to the States in 1988. Another married a Czech girl and went to live in Czechoslovakia. One married a Chinese girl and returned with her to the States in 1963 and another married in China but left his wife and returned in 1963 where he became an alcoholic and after six months in a psychiatric hospital died in 1995. The one who stayed was Private James Veneris who took a Chinese name and worked in a steel mill. He married three times, returned to the States in 1976 for a visit, but then went back to China where he died. Marine Andrew Condron from Perthshire, Scotland, married Jaquline, the daughter of a French Diplomat in Peking and returned to Scotland in 1963 where he found a job selling encyclopedias. After a Court of Enquiry, Condron was given an Honourable Discharge from the Navy, was not subjected to any disciplinary action and was paid for all the time he had served up to his discharge. The Americans were all given a Dishonourable Discharge but had to go to the Supreme Court before they received their pay up to the day of their Dishonourable Discharge.

During the war there was another example of the Chinese using prisoners for propaganda purposes. This was in connection with the claim that the Americans had used germ warfare. In the winter of 1950-51 there had been an outbreak of typhus among the Communists' forces which in part contributed to the failure of their Fifth Offensive. To explain the reason for this epidemic the Chinese alleged that the Americans had dropped bombs containing typhus germs. It was a great success, therefore, for the Communists to be able to broadcast interviews of thirty-six American airmen who admitted being involved in germ warfare. Lieutenant John Quinn was an important figure in this propaganda coup; he clearly believed he had been involved in germ warfare and was sent round the various camps to repeat his confession. Prisoners who heard him speak said he looked 'perfectly healthy' and added that there weren't any Chinese around him 'to make him say anything he didn't want to say.' Marine Colonel Frank H. Schwable signed a long and detailed confession describing his participation in germ warfare, all of which was nonsense. During the war in 1951, to discover the truth and to get a correct understanding of the typhus epidemic, a senior American Medical General was sent on a clandestine mission behind the Communist lines to take samples from the local population. His report confirmed typhus, but attributed the disease to poor hygiene and lack of adequate medical facilities. The Chinese allegations were, however, a cause of concern as they were repeated all over the world, particularly in Third World Countries. Even after their release many prisoners, including those who were not 'progressives', while scornful when describing the stories they had been told about the advantages of socialism over capitalism, admitted that they thought the Americans might have used germ warfare. In 2010 the Chinese initiated the rumour again alleging that as the Americans had used orange-defoliant and napalm to kill civilians in Vietnam and as they had developed germ warfare techniques during the Second World War, in the desperate period of the winter retreat in 1950 they might well have considered its use. However, no irrefutable evidence has ever been produced by Peking that the Americans did use germ warfare but the testimony of the prisoners helped in the deception.

The process of persuading prisoners to believe in lies came to be known as 'brainwashing'. It was not only the result of food deprivation and harsh conditions, but intense pressure over a long period in an environment where there are no contradictory opinions. The same effect can be achieved where young men live entirely in the closed world of a Christian or Buddhist religious seminary or a Moslem Madrassa. Constant repetition of facts, however distorted, can become an article of faith and can give the convert the deep satisfaction of having discovered the 'truth'. It was noticeable that the Chinese had no success in converting the Turkish prisoners to socialism and this was initially thought to be because of their religion and strong sense of patriotism. The conclusion was, however, that the Chinese did not have the capability in the Turkish language to maintain the continual verbal onslaught which is an essential part of the brainwashing process.

When the British captives returned home and the stories of the Chinese interrogation tactics emerged, a fresh look was taken at the then current Interrogation and Resistance to Interrogation Training. It was accepted that as those captured in Korea had not been prepared for brainwashing, training should be started to help anyone unfortunate enough to be captured in the future. It was important to emphasise that brainwashing need not succeed. Two men had earned the George Cross for proving this. Fusilier Derek Kinne of the Royal Northumberland Fusiliers refused to cooperate and was punished. Several times he was beaten to the point of unconsciousness, was kicked, prodded with bayonets, tied up for periods of twenty four hours, made to stand on tiptoes with a running noose around his neck so that if he slipped he would be throttled, and was in solitary confinement in a rat-infested 'kennel' for thirty days. The second was Lieutenant Terry Waters of the West Yorkshire Regiment attached to the Gloucestershire Regiment. His story has a particular poignancy as I had been on parade at Sandhurst when he had marched up the steps of the Old College to be commissioned. His bravery was not the result of adrenalin flow in the heat of battle or plain obstinacy when a captive, it was the act of a young man who, on his own, made a decision that cost him his life and saved the lives of his soldiers. After his capture, when he had been wounded in the Imjin Battle, the conditions he endured and the actions he took are covered in the *London Gazette* citation April 1954:

Lieutenant Waters and his men were imprisoned in a tunnel driven into the side of a hill through which a stream of water flowed continuously flooding a great deal of the floor in which were packed a great number of South Korean and European prisoners in rags, filthy and crawling with lice. In this cavern a number died daily from wounds, sickness or merely malnutrition; they were fed on two small meals of boiled maize daily. Of medical attention there was none. After a visit from a North Korean Political Officer who attempted to persuade them to volunteer to join a prisoner of war group known as 'Peace Fighters' with a promise of better food, of medical treatment and other benefits as a reward for such activity – an offer which they unanimously refused – Lieutenant Waters decided to order his men to pretend to accede to the offer in an effort to save their lives, giving the order to the senior rank in the British Party so that the men would act upon his order without fail. Realizing that they had failed to subvert the senior officer, the North Koreans now made a series of concerted efforts to persuade Lieutenant Waters to save himself by joining the camp. This he steadfastly refused to do and he died a short time after. He was a young inexperienced officer comparatively recently commissioned yet he set an example of the highest gallantry.

These two men had set a wonderful example, but training was now required to help soldiers in the event of being taken prisoner. The phenomenon of brainwashing raised considerable interest in scientific circles, and experiments were carried out in the United Kingdom and America on animals and humans to discover if the administration of electric shocks – inserting anodes into the brain – and use of hallucinogenic drugs could change patterns of behaviour and beliefs. Certain conclusions were reached and these conclusions have resulted in the use of anodes and drugs for legitimate medical treatment, for example in the treatment of Alzheimer's disease. But there is no evidence that the Chinese used these techniques on the prisoners of war. The new factor was the changed patterns of violence aimed at disorienting and confusing the prisoners then, by systematically reducing physical strength, inducing the prisoner to feel guilty, confess past errors and be ready, genuinely, to accept new political beliefs. The most significant remark by the returning prisoners was that they did not know what was happening and had no idea that they were going to be subjected to long periods of political indoctrination with the aim of using them for propaganda purposes. This had to be rectified and so the Ministry of Defence issued a new Conduct after Capture Training directive. This directive was for all three services and laid down that all servicemen would be given classroom instruction in Conduct after Capture by a unit officer or NCO who had first attended a three-day Resistance to Interrogation course. This course explained what might happen to a prisoner after his capture and what a Communist interrogator was hoping to achieve. It was all classroom instruction and no practical experience exercises were included. In addition to these courses, a second series of courses was run for a category of servicemen classed as 'Prone to Capture'. These included members of the Special Forces, certain Air Crew and Royal Naval Clearance Divers. The aim of this course was to enable the servicemen to experience the type of physical and psychological pressures that a Communist enemy might apply, and the effect these pressures would have. The practical exercises could include such Communist methods as constant hooding; deprivation of sleep; use of pressure positions when standing; lack of food; robust handling by guards and 'white sound' – a continual hissing sound played very loudly so that it blocks out all other sound and causes disorientation. Prisoners could be held for up to twenty-four hours with no more than eight hours actual interrogation, after which a senior exercise controller would carry out a debrief. This treatment could be quite an ordeal for prisoners, especially as it became part of the selection process for entry into the Special Forces, and before being captured they would have to take part in a two-day 'Escape and Evasion' exercise in locations like Dartmoor or the Yorkshire Moors where they would have little food or sleep. Before undertaking this training, all students were carefully briefed by the controlling staff including a doctor (psychiatrist) on the Communist methods of interrogation and what to expect if they were captured. They were also told that they could opt out of the Interrogation Phase of the exercise at any time if they felt unable to carry on by asking for the doctor or an umpire.

This practical course was quite separate from the Prisoner of War Handling and Tactical Questioning course where servicemen were taught the correct way to treat prisoners in line with the Geneva Convention and at the same time extract information at the point of capture.

The mistake made in the Northern Ireland conflict was in an operation called 'Motor Man' in which a large number of suspected terrorists or suspected terrorist sympathisers were arrested. In order to provide additional interrogation support the instructors from the Resistance to Interrogation team were sent to help the police. Some of the techniques they were using in their specialist Resistance to Interrogation training were incorrectly used in Northern Ireland – stress positions, hooding and white sound. When the public learned of the use of these techniques there was outrage and the Government ordered a three-man official enquiry headed by Lord Compton to carry out an investigation. The conclusion of the committee was that these methods were illegal and should be stopped. Interrogation was henceforth only conducted by policemen from the Royal Ulster Constabulary. This was a wise move as the British public became very uneasy about soldiers carrying out interrogations.

The Army was involved, however, in the guarding of prisoners held in the Maze Prison and here there are strong similarities between the situation on the Island of Koje-Do. In both countries the conflict arose out of an arbitrary line drawn across the country based on no natural geographic feature or simple ethnic divide. Whatever the cause, the result was bitter hatred between the two communities and, just as at Koje-Do where it was found to be sensible to separate Communists from non-Communists into their own compounds, so in the Maze it was sensible to separate Republicans from Loyalists. Just as in Koje-Do, there were internecine murders in the Maze Compounds, and just as in Koje-Do the segregation gave the hard-line elements the opportunity to recruit, indoctrinate and train new recruits. More importantly, just as at Koje-Do, prisoners in the Maze became a fruitful source of political propaganda. Orders for attempted escapes came from outside the prison and prisoners were encouraged to take extreme action in order to gain attention. Hunger strikes which led to suicides, and 'dirty protests' where prisoners smeared excrement on their walls, achieved great publicity and a great deal of sympathy from Republican supporters but, unlike at Koje-Do, when dealing with these problems the Security Forces did not degenerate into brutality; the response was firm but controlled.

The lesson of the Korean War that brutality was counter-productive matches the positive view of the British people that brutality is not acceptable and cannot be condoned. There have been two places in my life which stank of evil. One was in the Middle East, the other in the Far East. Both were places of interrogation, where in a dirty, dark cell a blood-stained wreck of a man crouched in a corner and another man in a sweat-stained vest shouted. Interrogation can bring out the worst in men; it can become a habit divorced from reality. Before any British soldier fills the role of interrogator, regardless of the circumstances, he must be trained in what is acceptable and then closely monitored by a senior command system. Interrogation of a prisoner is one of the finest ways of gaining information but it can lead to political repercussions that far outweigh the value of the information obtained.

Training is also necessary to prepare servicemen for capture. The past rule of number, rank, name and date of birth is still the best solution, but both the United States and British Army recognise that it is not possible to maintain this position when questioning lasts for long periods. Talk may be necessary but there are still rules: try not to antagonise, be aware of what the interrogator is trying to achieve, and never, never give the names of anybody. Since the Korean War, our servicemen have not had to suffer long periods of imprisonment but the experiences, fortitude and bravery of those made prisoner in Korea still provide guidelines for 'Conduct after Capture'.

The Korean War was the last time that the American Army or the Commonwealth armies took large numbers of prisoners of war. The governments involved recognised that it was a war and that therefore the requirements of the Geneva Convention were applicable. On the Island of Koje-Do, although the supervision of the guard force was initially not correct, representatives of the Red Cross were able to inspect the camps and there was international pressure from the United Nations and, in particular, the Commonwealth Counties that certain standards had to be maintained. There was also the very real situation that what happened on Koje-Do had a direct impact on the treatment of the United Nations prisoners held by China. The retrograde and sinister change that has happened since the Korean War is that in subsequent operations the respective governments have decided not to call their military operations a 'war', and that those who have been imprisoned are not therefore 'Prisoners of War'. Instead, a variety of other terms have been coined: 'terrorists, militants, insurgents, enemy combatants, rebels, fanatics, activists' – all titles which are used to obscure compliance with the obligations of the Geneva Convention. This policy may have had short-term advantages but abrogation of human rights for prisoners and allowing other nations to imprison those captured and giving them the right to carry out interrogations, has certainly had long-term adverse political repercussions. In the Korean War the handling of prisoners delayed the ceasefire for two years, but the lesson was not learned that if you go to war under whatever pretext or title, the same amount of manpower, skill and resources has to be put into prisoner handling as it is into tactical operations. Special Forces' successes and the killing of the enemy by sophisticated kinetic technology may give great satisfaction, but the success can be illusory. With the growth in media and communication capability and the growth of nationalistic and religious fervour, military success can be short-term if the civilian population retains hatred and the world believes that acts of inhumanity have been committed or condoned. In the Ministry of Defence document published in 1955 *Treatment of British Prisoners of War in Korea*, it states that Article 87 of the Geneva Convention provides that 'collective punishment for individual acts, corporal punishment, imprisonment in premises without daylight and in general any form of cruelty or torture are forbidden.' It is very disquieting and dangerous that the current practice of denying the requirements of the Geneva Convention to those who are captured in combat can be condoned on the grounds that the combat is not really a war.

CHAPTER TWENTY-ONE

Conclusion

A t the end of the Second World War the United States was confident about its military might. It had the greatest military capability the world had ever seen and had been victorious over Germany, Italy and Japan. In the post-war agreements, Russia, who had only entered the War days before the surrender of Japan, had negotiated at Potsdam the division of Korea into two separate entities. The line of demarcation was decided at fairly low level by US Military Officers in Okinawa thousands of miles away. It was a rough divide based on no other logic than being 'about halfway'. In the political vacuum that resulted, two men emerged determined to reunite their country. In the north it was Kim Il Sung who felt very comfortable with the Communist policies of Moscow; in the south it was Syngman Rhee who was determinedly nationalistic and who Washington found very difficult to deal with. For two years the United States wrestled with the complicated problems of South Korean internal politics trying to find a credible withdrawal formula. The solution they found in September 1947 was to refer the future of Korea to the United Nations and on 14 November 1947, the General Assembly, in spite of the objections of the Eastern Bloc countries, agreed that there was to be United Nations supervision of elections, followed by Korean independence and the withdrawal of all foreign forces. It was this decision by the United States to gain international support for their policies and involve the United Nations in the dispute that eventually led to the arrival of the Commonwealth Division in Korea and ultimately Baker Troop. In 1948, in line with the United Nations Resolution, the Russians agreed to withdraw their troops from Korea and the United States, albeit suspiciously, agreed to do the same. On 24 July 1948 the United States lowered their flag over the Capital Building in Seoul and the flag of the new South

Korean Republic was hoisted. All American troops withdrew except for a small Training and Advisory team. The Russians did not mind withdrawing; they were happy with their control over Kim Il Sung. The United States was happy to withdraw but was very unhappy with its control over the expansionist aims of Rhee, although MacArthur at the ceremony made the provocative statement: 'An artificial barrier had divided your land. This barrier must and shall be torn down.' It was a fine statement but, as the Russians and North Koreans rejected the electoral requirments for a unified Korea, the United Nations had no power to make them do so. The use of sanctions had not yet been developed and the only other option was the use of force, which, until the invasion of the South by the North, was not considered a realistic option.

By 1950 Russia had become the accepted main threat to the West. Washington and London were convinced that Stalin wished to convert, conquer and control as much of the world as possible. As both sides now had atomic weapons, defence was based on 'equal deterrence and mutual destruction' with the result that a major war had become unthinkable. Foreign policy, therefore, turned to prevention of the spread of Communism in areas where there was no risk of active military confrontation. To everyone's surprise Korea suddenly fell into this category. Whereas the United States had determinedly prevented Rhee from obtaining tanks, artillery and military aircraft and had made pretence of helping with training, Stalin had decided to re-arm Kim Il Sung and provided tanks, artillery and aircraft and had sent large numbers of experienced officers to help train the new Korean Communist Army. Washington had come to the conclusion that Stalin would never allow the North Koreans to attack a country supported by America and which contained US troops. Stalin had come to the conclusion that given the strength of the North Korean Army, the weakness of the South Korean Army, and the lukewarm support for Rhee by Washington, that a swift and powerful invasion could achieve victory and take possession of the whole of the Korean Peninsular. It was also thought to be highly unlikely that America would mobilise sufficient forces to launch an invasion to retake a Communist-controlled and well-armed Korea.

Only the United States had the power to save South Korea, and the decision of what to do fell to one man, President Truman. The occupation by Kim Il Sung of the Korean Peninsular posed no military threat to the United States. Any decision to send troops to Korea would not be based on any vital military necessity or any altruistic motive to protect the South Korean people; the aim would be to stop the spread of international Communism. This aim had the support of both the Democratic and Republican parties, in particular those politicians who actively supported the cause of Chiang Kai Shek and who felt the US had been humiliated by his defeat. Having come to the conclusion that action was required and having sent MacArthur to Korea to assess the situation, and received his recommendation that only the American military could prevent Korea from becoming Communist, he decided to send troops and involve his country in a new war. This he did with the agreement of both the Congress and the Senate. His next step, which was to result in the deaths of so many non-Americans, was to 'internationalise' his decision and ensnare the United Nations into agreement that the invasion by North Korea into South Korea was in breach of international law, could not be condoned and that a 'United Nations unified command should be established, led by General MacArthur with the aim of defeating the North Korean Army and restoring peace.' Prime Minister Attlee agreed with this conclusion and promised to provide military support, as did the Prime Ministers of Australia, Canada, New Zealand and South Africa and fifteen other countries. The unifying theme was that this was not a war, but a 'police action'. The commitment of forces was to be as token forces to show solidarity with the United Nations, not a declaration of war. It was a satisfying political gesture which conveniently forgot the reality on the ground of troops committed to battle. Commonwealth military chiefs were now ordered to send forces to an unknown country, to face an unknown enemy with unknown capability, without national armour, artillery, aircraft or intelligence support and with the minimum of national logistic support. The British plan was to form 29 Infantry Brigade from units in the UK and, when ready, send it to Korea via troop ship, but the situation in the Pusan Perimeter became critical and, as it was likely that by the time 29 Brigade arrived the

United Nations would have already been pushed into the sea, a quick decision was made on 19 August 1950 to send two infantry battalions brought up to war establishment by filleting three other battalions, four anti-tank guns, a Workshop and Ordnance Field Park from Hong Kong and call it 27 Infantry Brigade. The risks to the soldiers of sending them into the cauldron of the 'Pusan Perimeter' where one American division and three Korean Divisions had already suffered severe losses were immense. Army commanders have a natural inclination to obey orders; in 1950 there was no General Montgomery who several times aroused the wrath of his prime minister by refusing to commit his troops until he was sure of success. It is an enormous tribute to Brigadier Coad, the Argylls, the Middlesex, and then the 3rd Battalion Royal Australian Regiment and the New Zealand Artillery Regiment that on reaching Korea they adapted to the situation, maintained the momentum of their traditions and fought as a cohesive brigade.

At the United Nations level those countries that had agreed to join in the war had little or no influence as to how it was to be conducted. In Korea, senior United States officers made all the major decisions. The decisions to land at Inchon, to cross the 38th Parallel, to send troops up to the Yalu and to retreat were all made by General MacArthur. In spite of two grotesque intelligence mistakes, first concerning the North Korean invasion and second the crossing of Chinese troops into Korea, the Commonwealth Governments acquiesced to the war strategy decided by the United States, and in fact there was little point in their objecting. The Commonwealth Division was only one of over thirty American and ROK Divisions in Korea and the main sources of intelligence were controlled by the United States. The penalty for committing token forces to battle with a complete disregard for the lessons learned in the Second World War regarding armour, artillery and logistic support and relying on another country to provide this support, meant a loss of independent control and judgement which had fatal results for the Commonwealth forces.

At Divisional level, Lieutenant General Sir James Cassels, the Commonwealth Divisional Commander, made strenuous efforts to retain control, as he tactfully reported in a lecture to the Royal United

Services Institute in March 1953: 'I must admit, and the US commanders will I am sure agree, that we did have some awkward moments. Although in every case our aims were identical, our methods of achieving these aims were frequently quite different. It was natural for US commanders to expect to deal with me in exactly the same way as they would deal with any US Division. I of course, and my commanders below me, could not change our methods and I was quite determined that we would not change.'The main issue was that the Corps Commanders sometimes wished to use battalions of the Commonwealths Division in an independent role. This, of course, was not a problem for US battalions or battalions from countries such as Thailand, Costa Rica or the Philippines, but it was found to be very unsatisfactory to detach Commonwealth battalions from their brigade structures.

It is a traditional part of army life to believe your own unit is superior to any other; this applies at company level where, of course 'A' Company is better than 'B' Company and at battalion level where the idiosyncrasies and failures of other battalions are remembered over many generations. It is very satisfactory to report, therefore, that at the ground level there was a great deal of respect for the fighting ability and courage of the American servicemen. This is well demonstrated in the number of awards given to Americans during the Korean War. The number is impressive: two KCBs, five KBEs, eight CBs, thirty-four CBEs, fifteen OBEs, fourteen MBEs and four BEMs. Commander R. Budd US Navy was awarded the DSO for gallantry after taking his ship close inshore and providing rocket support. Eight men were awarded the Military Cross including Major G.D. Lamm who commanded the Special Forces (Guerrilla Division) and worked with Intelligence Corps Operatives behind the lines and Major K.W. Koch called by Farrar-Hockley 'The Intrepid Captain Koch' who, in the battle of Naktona River, continually led his tanks forward in support of the Commonwealth troops. His citation reads: 'This officer's personal courage and leadership brings great credit to himself, his Service and his country.' In the same battle, Captain H. Moore, US Army Artillery, also earned the Military Cross as he continually moved his guns in close support of 27 Brigade and'when enemy guns were storming his position he ordered his 105mm howitzers to be brought into action and used as direct fire weapons.' Three other Military Crosses went to helicopter pilots of the US Air Force. One citation to Captain E.L. MacQuarrie reads: 'In response to a ground signal from a British soldier, in broad daylight and despite intense enemy small arms fire directed against him, Captain MacQuarrie landed his helicopter and, showing the utmost calmness and courage, personally and unaided, evacuated two wounded soldiers back to safety.' Another Military Cross went to a US Air Force paramedic. A British fighter plane had crashed and Captain Shumate was part of the rescue helicopter team. 'He left the helicopter upon landing and rushed to the aid of the pilot. Enemy forces from a nearby farm opened fire in an attempt to prevent any aid. At the risk of his life Captain Shumate leaped onto the wing of the aircraft and attempted to lift the pilot out of the cockpit. The pilot, paralysed from the waist down was pinned to the wreckage by his flying suit and still under enemy fire. Captain Shumate lifted and held the pilot with one arm and with his free hand cut away the pilot's flying suit and managed to drag him to safety. The injured British fighter pilot was placed aboard and flown to hospital. The gallantry displayed by Captain Shumate was in keeping with the highest traditions of the military service and reflects great credit upon himself and the United States Air Force.' In addition to these gallantry awards to the US Army and the US Air Force, there were ten awards for the US Navy of DFCs including two with a second award bar, nine DSCs, seven DSMs and a DFM. Whatever the failings at strategic level and whatever the failing in intelligence, in close combat American servicemen proved time and time again to their Allies that they were skilful, courageous and determined.

What of the Royal Artillery, 20th Field Regiment RA and Baker Troop in particular? It is quietly satisfying to report that 'we did our job.' No great dramatics, but when required we were in position, we were trained, we fired some sixty thousand rounds, and time and time again the Infantry battalions expressed gratitude that the accuracy and rate of our fire prevented the enemy from overrunning their trenches.

There were over 100,000 men fighting on behalf of the United Nations who had been killed in the Korean War. Over one million

South Koreans, both military and civilian, also lost their lives. Among the 1,078 British dead were 75 members of the Royal Artillery including the seven from 20 Field Regiment RA. Standing looking at the graves in the beautifully kept Commonwealth Cemetery in Pusan, and in particular at the graves of Captain Bill Miller and Bombardier Ken Alder, the two gunners killed with the Duke of Wellington's Regiment on The Hook, and the three King's men who died on the night of the Warsaw Cave Raid, there was good reason to reflect as to whether their deaths were worthwhile.

Soldiers who served in Korea for twenty-four hours between 2nd July 1950 and 27 July 1953 were awarded the Queen's Korea Medal and the United Nations Korea Service Medal, while later arrivals who served until 27 Jul 1954 received the United Nations Medal only. Over the next thirty-five years soldiers who fought in Korea could qualify for the General Service Medal 1918-62 in the campaigns of Malaya, Canal Zone, Cyprus, Near East, Arabian Peninsular and Brunei, and then the General Service Medal 1962 for campaigns in Borneo, Radfan, South Arabia, Canal Zone, Borneo, Radfan, South Arabia, Malay Peninsular, South Vietnam, Northern Ireland, Dhofar, Lebanon, N. Iraq and S. Turkey and Air Operations in Iraq, Kuwait, Northern Ireland, Dhofar and Lebanon. Other medals could be earned for service in Rhodesia and the Falklands. It is a remarkable catalogue of campaigns for a period when theoretically Britain was at peace.

In many of these campaigns Britain was fighting battles which arose from the turbulent period of 'giving up an Empire'. The aim of the British Government was to fill the vacuum left by their departure by establishing a democratic government and a good administration. Not surprisingly, competing factions arose in each state where the prize was the control of an independent country and fighting erupted. In retrospect the British soldiers who lost their lives trying to ensure a peaceful handover did die in a worthwhile cause and what were previously called Newly Emergent States are now established as independent members of the United Nations.

It is also gratifying to record that all those concerned, the British Colonial Officers, the Colonial Police and the members of all three services managed to cope with difficult and dangerous situations where all sides suffered deaths, but managed to hand over the colonies without leaving a residual legacy of hatred. It is perhaps only the Falklands and Korea where the fighting was to save a country from occupation. The Falklands remains with a freedom that is the overwhelming wish of the inhabitants and South Korea is internationally accepted as a democratic state with a vibrant economy and is a remarkable example of freedom in the Far East. Everybody who was in Korea between 1950 and 1953 is amazed that the devastation and violent disruption of that time has so dramatically improved, and this incredible improvement is made more striking when a comparison is made with the poverty, depression and dictatorship in North Korea. The conclusion must be that in the Korean War the soldiers did die in a worthwhile cause.

Since Korea, it has become a pattern in many independent countries that the sacrifices of the British servicemen have been white-washed from local history. Independent countries find it embarrassing to recognise the contribution that our servicemen made to give them this independence. To the young of these countries the campaigns which qualified for the clasps to the General Service Medal seem as remote as 1066 to the British. The exceptions are the battles of Korea and the Falklands. Korea was a worthwhile cause; it stopped the militant Communist dictatorship of Stalin and the ideological dictatorship of Mao. It is remembered by the people of South Korea and that is why Korean veterans of all nations are so proud to have participated.

Bibliography

Adams Della and Lewis H. Carlson, *An American Dream*, USA 2007

Anderson E., *Banner over Pusan*, England 1960

Barker A.J., *Fortune Favours The Brave*, Great Britain 1974

Borch F.L. and Westlake W.R., *For Heroic or Meritorious Achievement*, Arizona, USA 1995

Brady James, *The Coldest War*, USA 1990

Breuer William B., *Shadow Warriors*, USA 1996

Burrill David, *Prisoners Intelligence and War* 1990

Bussey Charles M., *Firefight at Yechon*, USA 1991

Carew Tim, *The Commonwealth at War*, London 1967

Cunningham Cyril, *No Mercy No Leniency*, Great Britain 2000

Cunningham-Booth A. and Farrar P., *British Forces in Korea*, UK 1988

Davies S.J., *In Spite of Dungeons*, Great Britain 1954

Doherty Richard, *The Sons of Ulster*, Belfast 2008

Durney James, *The Far Side of the World*, Leinester, Naas, 2005

Farrar-Hockley A., *The British Part in the Korean War Vol 1*, UK 1990

Farrar-Hockley A., *The British Part in the Korean War Vol 11*, UK 1995

Fisher Peter and Lohan Patrick, *In Memoriam*, England 2006

Forty George, *At War in Korea*, London 1982

Gaston Peter, *The 38th Parallel*, Glasgow 1976

Gaston Peter, *Korea Prisoners of War The British Army*, London 1976

Green David, *Captured at the Imjin River*, Great Britain 2003

Halberstam David, *The Coldest Winter*, Great Britain 2007

Harding E.D., *The Imjin Roll*, Gloucester, England 1976

Harris A.M., *Grains of Sand*, Australia 1968

Hastings Max, *The Korean War*, London 1987

H.M. Government, *Treatment of British Prisoners of War in Korea*, 1955

Hickey Michael, *Korean War: The West Confronts Communism 1950-1953*, John Murray 1999

Holroyd Reuban, *Moving On*, Halifax, England 1964

Jackson Robert, *Air War Over Korea*, London 1973

Langley Michael, *Inchon MacArthur's Last Triumph*, London 1979

Larby Ron, *Signals to the Right Armoured Corps to the Left,* UK 1993

Large Lofty, *One Man's War in Korea,* England 1988

Large Lofty, *Soldier against the Odds,* Great Britain 1999

Linklater Eric, *Our Men in Korea,* H.M. Stationery Office 1952

Malcolm G.I., *The Argylls in Korea,* Edinburgh, Scotland 1952

Mock John T., *Naval Honours for Korea,* England 1992

Morrissey P.B. and Westlake W.R., *British Orders and Medals awarded to American Forces for the Korean War,* USA 2003

Moskin J. Robert, *Turncoat,* USA 1966

Naval and Military Press, *Casualties Sustained by the British Army in the Korean War 1950-53,* England.

Newcombe Michael, *Guns and the Morning Calm,* England 1999

Odgers George, *Across The Parallel,* Melbourne, Australia 1953

Owen Colin R., *The South African Korea Medal Roll,* South Africa 1982

Parritt B.A.H., *The Intelligencers,* England 2011

Pasley Virginia, *22 Stayed,* London 1955

Rees David, *The Korean War History and Tactics,* London 1984

Salmon Andrew, *To The Last Round,* Great Britain 2009

Spur Russell, *Enter the Dragon,* Newmarket Press, N.Y. 1988

Stone I.F., *The Hidden History of the Korean War,* USA 1952

Terry Addison, *The Battle for Pusan,* USA 2000

Trigg Noel, *A Different Kind Of Fighting,* Newport Printing Company, Wales

Waller Brigadier H.J. de, *History of the Royal Regiment of Artillery,* UK

War Diaries 20th Field Regiment RA Firepower Museum Woolwich, UK

Whatmore D.E., *One Road to Imjin,* Chippenham, England 1993

Whiting Charles, *Battleground Korea,* United Kingdom 1999.

Williams Newville, *A Conscript in Korea,* Barnsley, England, 2009

Willoughby Charles A. and Chamberlain J., *MacArthur 1941-1951,* Great Britain 1956

Xiaobing Li, *Mao's Generals Remember Korea,* University Press of Kansas, 2001

Index